"America's leading source of self-help legal information." ★★★★
—YAHOO!

LEGAL INFORMATION ONLINE ANYTIME

24 hours a day

www.nolo.com

AT THE NOLO.COM SELF-HELP LAW CENTER, YOU'LL FIND

- **Nolo's comprehensive Legal Encyclopedia** filled with plain-English information on a variety of legal topics
- **Nolo's Law Dictionary**—legal terms <u>without</u> the legalese
- **Auntie Nolo**—if you've got questions, Auntie's got answers
- **The Law Store**—over 200 self-help legal products including Downloadable Software, Books, Form Kits and eGuides
- **Legal and product updates**
- **Frequently Asked Questions**
- **NoloBriefs,** our free monthly email newsletter
- **Legal Research Center,** for access to state and federal statutes
- **Our ever-popular lawyer jokes**

Quality LAW BOOKS & SOFTWARE FOR EVERYONE

Nolo's user-friendly products are consistently first-rate. Here's why:

- A dozen in-house legal editors, working with highly skilled authors, ensure that our products are accurate, up-to-date and easy to use
- We continually update every book and software program to keep up with changes in the law
- Our commitment to a more democratic legal system informs all of our work
- We appreciate & listen to your feedback. Please fill out and return the card at the back of this book.

OUR "NO-HASSLE" GUARANTEE

Return anything you buy directly from Nolo for any reason and we'll cheerfully refund your purchase price. No ifs, ands or buts.

Read This First

The information in this book is as up to date and accurate as we can make it. But it's important to realize that the law changes frequently, as do fees, forms and procedures. If you handle your own legal matters, it's up to you to be sure that all information you use—including the information in this book—is accurate. Here are some suggestions to help you:

First, make sure you've got the most recent edition of this book. To learn whether a later edition is available, check the edition number on the book's spine and then go to Nolo's online Law Store at www.nolo.com or call Nolo's Customer Service Department at 800-728-3555.

Next, even if you have a current edition, you need to be sure it's fully up to date. The law can change overnight. At www.nolo.com, we post notices of major legal and practical changes that affect the latest edition of a book. To check for updates, find your book in the Law Store on Nolo's website (you can use the "A to Z Product List" and click the book's title). If you see an "Updates" link on the left side of the page, click it. If you don't see a link, that means we haven't posted any updates. (But check back regularly.)

Finally, we believe accurate and current legal information should help you solve many of your own legal problems on a cost-efficient basis. But this text is not a substitute for personalized advice from a knowledgeable lawyer. If you want the help of a trained professional, consult an attorney licensed to practice in your state.

4th edition

Leases & Rental Agreements

by Marcia Stewart and Attorneys Ralph Warner
& Janet Portman

FOURTH EDITION	June 2003
COVER DESIGN	Toni Ihara
BOOK DESIGN	Terri Hearsh
INDEX	Julie Shawvan
PROOFREADING	Joe Sadusky
PRINTING	Consolidated Printers, Inc.

Stewart, Marcia.
    Leases & rental agreements / by Marcia Stewart & Janet Portman & Ralph Warner. -- 4th ed.
      p. cm.
    Includes index.
    ISBN 0-87337-941-1
     1. Leases--United States--Popular works. 2. Landlord and tenant--United
States--Popular works. I. Title: Leases and rental agreements. II. Warner, Ralph E. III.
Portman, Janet. IV. Title.

KF590.Z9S744 2003
346.7304'346--dc21

                                           2003042240

For information on bulk purchases or corporate premium sales, please contact the Special
Sales Department. For academic sales or textbook adoptions, ask for Academic Sales. Call
800-955-4775 or write to Nolo at 950 Parker Street, Berkeley, CA 94710.

Acknowledgments

Special thanks to Mary Randolph, editor and friend extraordinaire, who contributed many valuable ideas to this book.

Many other Nolo colleagues and friends helped with this book. Special thanks to: Ella Hirst and Stan Jacobsen for their cheerful and meticulous research assistance; Amy Ihara, Terri Hearsh, Toni Ihara and Margaret Livingston for their creative and skillful book design; and Susan Putney and Jaleh Doane, who always make the book production process go so smoothly.

Table of Contents

4 Getting the Tenant Moved In

5 Changing or Ending a Tenancy

Appendices

1 State Landlord-Tenant Law Charts

State Landlord-Tenant Statutes

Notice Required to Change or Terminate a Month-to-Month Tenancy

State Rent Rules

State Security Deposit Rules

States That Require Landlords to Maintain a Separate Account for Security Deposits

States That Require Landlords to Pay Interest on Deposits

Attachment to Florida Leases and Rental Agreements (Security Deposits)

State Laws on Landlord's Access to Rental Property

2 Tear-Out Forms

Index

CHAPTER

1

Being a Successful Landlord

The rental agreement or lease that you and your tenant sign is the contractual basis of your relationship. Taken together with the landlord-tenant laws of your state—and, in a few areas, local and federal laws—it sets out almost all the legal rules you and your tenant must follow. Your rental agreement or lease is also an immensely practical document, full of crucial business details, such as how long the tenant can occupy your property and the amount of the rent.

Given their importance, there's no question that you need to create effective and legal rental agreements or leases with your tenants. This book shows you how, by providing clearly written, fair and effective tear-out lease and rental agreement forms, along with clear explanations of each clause.

Our agreements are legally accurate and up to date, based on careful research of every state's landlord-tenant laws. They can be tailored to fit the details of your situation using the 50–state law charts in Appendix 1. Throughout the book, we suggest ways to do this and also caution you about the types of modifications likely to get you into legal hot water.

In addition to showing you how to prepare a lease or rental agreement, this book also covers key legal issues that landlords need to understand, including how to legally choose tenants and start a tenancy. It also highlights the legal and practical issues involved with changing or ending a tenancy. This book provides forms that supplement a lease and a rental agreement, including a rental application designed to help you choose the best tenant. Other forms, such as a Landlord/Tenant Checklist (used to document the condition of the rental unit at the beginning and end of the tenancy), will help you avoid legal problems with tenants such as disputes over security deposits.

⚠️ Who shouldn't use our lease or rental agreement?

Don't use the forms in this book if you're renting out property that is subsidized by the government, such as the Section 8 program of the federal Department of Housing and Urban Development. You may need to use a special government-drafted lease. Also, our forms should not be used for renting out mobile homes, townhouses, hotels or commercial property. If you are renting out your condominium or townhouse, use this book in conjunction with your homeowners' associations's rules and regulations (called CC&Rs, or covenants, codes and restrictions). These CC&Rs may affect how you structure the terms and conditions of the rental.

Every Landlord's Legal Guide

A lease or rental agreement is only one part of a landlord-tenant legal relationship. For example, many state (and some federal and local) laws are also extremely important. A comprehensive explanation of these laws, and the practical steps rental property owners can take to comply with them (while at the same time running an efficient and profitable business), is covered in *Every Landlord's Legal Guide,* by Marcia Stewart, Ralph Warner & Janet Portman (Nolo).

Every Landlord's Legal Guide covers most key laws affecting landlords in all 50 states, including your repair and maintenance responsibilities and your liability for crime and environmental hazards such as lead. *Every Landlord's Legal Guide* covers rules and procedures for collecting and returning security deposits, anti-discrimination laws, privacy rules, employment laws affecting managers, how to resolve problems with tenants or begin the eviction process and more. It includes over 20 legal forms on CD and in tear-out form.

You can order *Every Landlord's Legal Guide* from Nolo's website (www.nolo.com) or by phone (800-728-3555). You can also find Nolo books at bookstores and public libraries.

Ten Tips for Being a Successful Landlord

1. **Don't rent to anyone before checking his credit history, references and background.** Haphazard screening too often results in problems—a tenant who pays the rent late or not at all, trashes your place or moves in undesirable friends—or worse.

2. **Get all the important terms of the tenancy in writing.** Beginning with the rental application and lease or rental agreement, be sure to document important facts of your relationship with your tenants—including when and how you handle tenant complaints and repair problems, notice you must give to enter a tenant's apartment and the like.

3. **Establish a clear, fair system of setting, collecting, holding and returning security deposits.** Inspect and document the condition of the rental unit before the tenant moves in to avoid disputes over security deposits when the tenant moves out.

4. **Stay on top of repair and maintenance needs and make repairs when requested.** If the property is not kept in good repair, you'll alienate good tenants. And they may have the right to withhold rent, sue for any injuries caused by defective conditions or move out without notice.

5. **Don't let your tenants and property be easy marks for a criminal.** You could well be liable for the tenant's losses. Landlords are sued more than any other group of business owners in the country. The average settlement paid by a landlord's insurance company is $600,000, and the average jury award is $1.2 million.

6. **Respect your tenants' privacy.** Notify tenants whenever you plan to enter their rental unit, and provide as much notice as possible, at least 24 hours or the minimum amount required by state law.

7. **Disclose environmental hazards such as lead.** Landlords are increasingly being held liable for tenant health problems resulting from exposure to environmental poisons in the rental premises.

8. **Choose and supervise your manager carefully.** If a manager commits a crime or is incompetent, you may be held financially responsible. Do a thorough background check and clearly spell out the manager's duties to help prevent problems down the road.

9. **Purchase enough liability and other property insurance.** A well-designed insurance program can protect your rental property from losses caused by everything from fire and storms to burglary, vandalism and personal injury and discrimination lawsuits.

10. **Try to resolve disputes with tenants without lawyers and lawsuits.** If you have a conflict with a tenant over rent, repairs, your access to the rental unit, noise or some other issue that doesn't immediately warrant an eviction, meet with the tenant to see if the problem can be resolved informally. If that doesn't work, consider mediation by a neutral third party, often available at little or no cost from a publicly funded program. If your dispute involves money and all attempts to reach agreement fail, try small claims court, where you can represent yourself. Use it to collect unpaid rent or to seek money for property damage after a tenant moves out and the deposit is exhausted.

Icons Used in This Book

Related Topics
This icon refers you to organizations, books or other resources for more information about the particular issue or topic discussed in the text.

Warning
Slow down and consider potential problems you may encounter when renting out residential property.

Fast Track
You may be able to skip some material that doesn't apply to your situation.

Form in Appendix
A blank, tear-out copy of the form discussed in the text is in Appendix 2.

Tip
A practical tip or good idea.

Rent Control
A rent control ordinance may address the issue discussed in the text.

Briefcase
You probably need the advice of a lawyer who specializes in landlord-tenant law.

Get a Little Help From Your Friends

Many landlords have discovered the value of belonging to a local or state association of rental property owners. These organizations range from small, volunteer-run groups to substantial city, county or even statewide organizations with paid staff and lobbyists. Many offer a wide variety of support and services to their members, including the following:

- legal information and updates through newsletters, publications, seminars and other means
- tenant screening and credit check services
- training and practical advice on compliance with legal responsibilities
- a place to meet other rental property owners and exchange information and ideas, and
- referrals to knowledgeable and appropriately priced professionals, including attorneys, accountants, maintenance firms and property management companies.

If you can't find an association of rental property owners in your phone book, ask other landlords for references. You can also contact the National Apartment Association (NAA), a national organization whose members include many individual state associations:

National Apartment Association
201 North Union Street, Suite 200
Alexandria, VA 22314
703-518-6141
www.naahq.org

The National Multi-Housing Council, a national organization of many of the country's largest landlords, may also be helpful:

National Multi-Housing Council
1850 M Street, NW, Suite 540
Washington, DC 20036
202-974-2300
www.nmhc.org

Preparing a Lease or Rental Agreement

This chapter provides step-by-step instructions on how to prepare a lease or rental agreement form. It discusses important issues that relate to your choices—as to both the type of document and the specific provisions—including any state, federal and local laws that may apply.

The lease and rental agreement forms are legally sound as designed.
If you change important terms or make major changes, however, you may affect a form's legal validity. In this case, you may wish to have your work reviewed by an experienced landlords' lawyer.

A. Which Is Better, a Lease or a Rental Agreement?

One of the key decisions you need to make is whether to use a lease or a rental agreement. Often, but by no means always, your choice will depend on how long you want a tenant to stay. But, since other factors can also come into play, read what follows carefully before evaluating your own situation and making a decision.

1. Month-to-Month Rental Agreement

A written rental agreement provides for a tenancy for a short period of time. The law refers to these agreements as periodic or month-to-month tenancies, although it is often legally possible to base them on other time periods, as would be the case if the rent must be paid every two weeks. A month-to-month tenancy automatically renews each month—or other agreed-upon period—unless the landlord or tenant gives the other the proper amount of written notice (typically 30 days) and terminates the agreement.

Month-to-month rental agreements give you more flexibility than leases. You may increase the rent or change other terms of the tenancy on relatively short notice (subject to any restrictions of local rent control ordinances—see sidebar, "Rent Control," below). And with proper notice, you may also end the tenancy at any time (again, subject to any rent control restrictions). (Chapter 5 discusses notice requirements to change or end a rental agreement.) Not surprisingly, many landlords prefer to rent month to month, particularly in urban areas with tight rental markets where new tenants are usually easily found and rents are trending upwards.

On the flip side, a month-to-month tenancy almost guarantees more tenant turnover. Tenants who may legally move out with only 30 days' notice may be more inclined to do so than tenants who make a longer commitment. Some landlords base their rental business strategy on painstakingly seeking high-quality, long-term renters. If you're one of those, or if you live in an area where it's difficult to fill vacancies, you will probably want tenants to commit for a longer period, such as a year. As discussed below, a fixed-term lease, especially when combined with tenant-friendly management policies, may encourage tenants to stay longer. However, it is no guarantee against turnover.

2. Fixed-Term Lease

A lease is a contract that obligates both you and the tenant for a set period of time—usually six months or a year, but sometimes longer. With a fixed-term lease, you can't raise the rent or change other terms of the tenancy until the lease runs out, unless the lease itself allows future changes or the tenant agrees in writing to the changes.

In addition, you usually can neither ask a tenant to move out nor prevail in an eviction lawsuit before the lease term expires unless the tenant fails to pay the rent or violates another significant term of the lease or state law, such as repeatedly making too much noise, damaging the rental unit or selling drugs on your property. This restriction can sometimes be problematic if you end up with a tenant you would like to be rid of but don't have sufficient cause to evict.

To take but one example, if you wish to sell the property halfway into the lease, the existence of long-term tenants—especially if they are paying less than the market rate—may be a negative factor. The new owner usually purchases all the obligations of the previous owner, including the obligation to honor existing leases. Of course, the opposite can also be true: If you have good, long-term tenants paying a fair rent, the property may be very attractive to potential new owners.

At the end of the lease term, you have several options. You can:

- decline to renew the lease, except in the few areas where local rent control requirements prohibit it
- sign a new lease for a set period, or
- do nothing—which means, under the law of most states, your lease will usually turn into a month-to-month tenancy if you continue to accept monthly rent from the tenant.

(Chapter 5 discusses in more detail how fixed-term leases end.)

Although leases restrict your flexibility, there's often a big plus to having long-term tenants. Some tenants make a serious personal commitment when they enter into a long-term lease, in part because they think they'll be liable for several months' rent if they leave early. And people who plan to be with you over the long term are often more likely to respect your property and the rights of other tenants, making the management of your rental units far easier and more pleasant.

⚠️ A lease guarantees less income security than you think.

As experienced landlords know well, it's usually not hard for a determined tenant to break a lease and avoid paying all of the money theoretically owed for the unused portion of the lease term. A few states allow tenants to break a lease without penalty in specific circumstances, such as the need to move to a care facility. (In addition, tenants who enter military service are entitled to break a lease, as explained in the sidebar "Special Rules for Tenants Who Enter Military Service" in Chapter 5, Section

B.). And many states require landlords to "mitigate" (minimize) the loss they suffer as a result of a broken lease—meaning that if a tenant moves out early, you must try to find another suitable tenant at the same or a greater rent. If you re-rent the unit immediately (or if a judge believes it could have been re-rented with a reasonable effort), the lease-breaking tenant is off the hook—except, perhaps, for a small obligation to pay for the few days or weeks the unit was vacant plus any costs you incurred in re-renting it. (Chapter 5, Section C, discusses a landlord's responsibility to mitigate damages if the tenant leaves early.)

As mentioned, you'll probably prefer to use leases in areas where there is a high vacancy rate or it is difficult to find tenants for one season of the year. For example, if you are renting near a college that is in session for only nine months a year, or in a vacation area that is deserted for months, you are far better off with a year's lease. This is especially true if you have the market clout to charge a large deposit, so that a tenant who wants to leave early has an incentive to find someone to take over the tenancy.

💡 Always put your agreement in writing.

Oral leases or rental agreements are perfectly legal for month-to-month tenancies and for leases of a year or less in most states. While oral agreements are easy and informal, it is never wise to use one. As time passes, people's memories (even yours) have a funny habit of becoming unreliable. You can almost count on tenants claiming that you made, but didn't keep, certain oral promises—for example, to repaint their kitchen or to not increase the rent. Tenants may also forget their own key agreements, such as no subletting. And other issues—for example, how deposits may be used—probably aren't covered at all. Oral leases are especially dangerous, because they require that both parties accurately remember one important term—the length of the lease—over a considerable time. If something goes wrong with an oral rental agreement or lease, you and your tenants are all too likely to end up in court, arguing over who said what to whom, when and in what context.

B. Completing the Lease or Rental Agreement Form

This section explains each clause in the lease and rental agreement forms that are provided in this book. Both forms cover the basic terms of the tenancy (such as the amount of rent and date due). Except for Clause 4, Term of the Tenancy, the lease and rental agreement forms are identical.

You may be tempted to simply tear out the form you use from the back of this book and skip over detailed instructions. This would be a mistake. If there is one area of landlord-tenant law where details count, this is it. Make sure you really do have the information necessary to create a lease or a rental agreement that accurately reflects your business strategy and complies with all the laws of your state.

Appendix 2 includes blank tear-out versions of the Month-to-Month Rental Agreement and the Fixed-Term Residential Lease (in English and in Spanish). A filled-in sample rental agreement is shown at the end of this chapter.

How to Prepare Attachment Pages

Although we have tried to leave adequate blank space on the forms, it's possible that you may run out of room in completing a particular clause, or you may want to add a clause. If you need to add anything to your lease or rental agreement, take the following steps:

1. At the first place that you run out of room, begin your entry and then write "Continued on Attachment 1." Similarly, if there is another place where you run out of room, add as much material as you can and then write "Continued on Attachment 2," and so on. Use a separate Attachment each time you need more space.

2. Make your own Attachment form, using a sheet of blank white paper. At the top of the form, fill in the proper number—that is, "Attachment 1" for the first attachment, and so on.

3. Begin each Attachment with the number of the clause you're continuing or adding. Then add "a continuation of" if you're continuing a clause, or "an addition to" if you're adding a clause.

4. Type or print the additional information on the Attachment.

5. Both you and each tenant should sign the page at the end of the added material.

6. Staple the Attachment page to the lease or rental agreement.

Clause 1.   Identification of Landlord and Tenant

This Agreement is entered into between

_____ ("Tenant") and

_____ ("Landlord").

Each Tenant is jointly and severally liable for the payment of rent and performance of all other terms of this Agreement.

Every lease or rental agreement must identify the tenant and the landlord or property owner—usually called the "parties" to the agreement. The term "Agreement" (a synonym for contract) refers to either the lease or the rental agreement.

Any competent adult—at least 18 years of age—may be a party to a lease or rental agreement. (A teenager under age 18 may also be a party to a lease if he or she has achieved legal adult status through a court order, military service or marriage.)

The last sentence of Clause 1 states that if you have more than one tenant, they (the cotenants) are all "jointly and severally" liable for paying rent and abiding by all the terms of the agreement. This essential bit of legalese simply means that each tenant is legally responsible for the whole rent and complying with the lease. This part of the clause gives you important rights; it means you can legally seek the entire rent from any one of the tenants should the others skip out or be unable to pay. A "jointly and severally liable" clause also gives you the right to evict all of the tenants even if just one has broken the terms of the lease—for example, by seriously damaging the property, or moving in an extra roommate or a dog, contrary to the lease or a rental agreement.

How to Fill In Clause 1:

Fill in the names of all tenants—adults who will live in the premises, including both members of a married couple. It's crucial that everyone who lives in your rental unit signs the lease or the rental agreement. This underscores your expectation that each individual is responsible for the

rent and the use of the property. Also, make sure the tenant's name matches his or her legal documents, such as a driver's license. You may set a reasonable limit on the number of people per rental unit. (See sidebar, "How Many Occupants to Allow," below.)

In the last blank, list the names of all landlords or property owners.

Chapter 3 provides detailed advice on choosing tenants.

Clause 2.   Identification of Premises

Subject to the terms and conditions in this Agreement, Landlord rents to Tenant, and Tenant rents from Landlord, for residential purposes only, the premises located at

_____ ("the premises"),

together with the following furnishings and appliances:

_____

_____ .

Rental of the premises also includes _____

_____ .

Clause 2 identifies the location of the property being rented (the premises) and provides details on furnishings. The words "for residential purposes only" are to prevent a tenant from using the property for conducting a business that might affect your insurance or violate zoning laws.

How to Fill In Clause 2:

Fill in the address of the unit or house you are renting. If there is an apartment or building number, specify that as well as the city and state.

Add as much detail as necessary to clarify what's included in—or excluded from—the rental premises, such as kitchen appliances. If the rental unit is fully furnished, state that here and provide detailed information on the Landlord/Tenant Checklist included in Chapter 4.

In some circumstances, you may want to elaborate on exactly what the premises include. For example, if the rental unit includes a parking space, storage in the garage or basement or other use of the property, such as a gardening shed in the backyard or the use of a barn in rural areas, specifically include it in your description of the premises. (See sidebar, "How to Prepare Attachment Pages," at the beginning of this section.)

Possible Modifications to Clause 2:

If a particular part of the rental property that a tenant might reasonably assume to be included is not being rented, such as a garage or storage shed you wish to use yourself or rent to someone else, explicitly exclude it from your description of the premises.

⚠️ Investigate before letting a tenant run a business on the premises.

Over twenty million Americans run a business from their house or apartment. If a tenant asks you to modify Clause 2 to allow him to operate a business, you have some checking to do—even if you are disposed to say yes. For starters, you'll need to check local zoning laws for restrictions on home-based businesses, including the type of businesses allowed (if any), the amount of car and truck traffic the business can generate, outside signs, on-street parking, the number of employees and the percentage of floor space devoted to the business. You'll also want to consult your insurance company as to whether you'll need a more expensive policy to cover the potential liability of employees or guests. In many situations, a home office for occasional use will not be a problem. But if the tenant wants to operate a business that involves people and deliveries coming and going, such as a therapy practice, jewelry importer or small business consulting firm, you should seriously consider whether to expand or add coverage. You may also want to require that the tenant maintain certain types of liability insurance,

so that you won't wind up paying if someone gets hurt on the rental property—for example, a business customer who trips and falls on the front steps. Also, be aware that if you allow a residence to be used as a commercial site, your property may need to meet the accessibility requirements of the federal Americans With Disabilities Act (commonly known as the ADA). For more information on the ADA, contact the U.S. Department of Justice, Office on the Americans With Disabilities Act, Civil Rights Division, in Washington, DC, at 800-514-0301, or check their website at www.usdoj.gov/crt/ada/adahom1.htm.

Clause 3. Limits on Use and Occupancy

The premises are to be used only as a private residence for Tenant(s) listed in Clause 1 of this Agreement, and their minor children. Occupancy by guests for more than _____ is prohibited without Landlord's written consent and will be considered a breach of this Agreement.

Clause 3 specifies that the rental unit is only the residence of the tenants and their minor children. It lets the tenants know that they may not move anyone else in as a permanent resident without your consent. The value of this clause is that a tenant who tries to move in a relative or friend for a longer period has clearly violated a defined standard, which gives you grounds for eviction. (New York landlords, however, are subject to the "Roommates Law," RPL 235-f, which allows tenants to move in relatives and other qualified individuals. The number of total occupants is still restricted, however, by local laws governing overcrowding.)

Clause 3 also includes a time limit for guest stays. Even if you do not plan to strictly enforce restrictions on guests, this provision will be very handy if a tenant tries to move in a friend or relative for a month or two, calling her a guest. It will give you the leverage you need to ask the guest to leave, request that the guest become a tenant with an appropriate increase in rent or, if necessary, evict the tenant for violating this lease provision.

How to Fill In Clause 3:

Fill in the number of days you allow guests to stay without your consent. We suggest you allow up to ten days in any six-month period, but, of course, you may want to modify this based on your own experience.

⚠ *Don't discriminate against families with children.*

You can legally establish reasonable space-to-people ratios, but you cannot use overcrowding as an excuse for refusing to rent to tenants with children, especially if you would rent to the same number of adults. (See sidebar, "How Many Tenants to Allow," below.) Discrimination against families with children is illegal, except in housing reserved for senior citizens only. Just as important as adopting a reasonable people-to-square foot standard in the first place is the maintenance of a consistent occupancy policy. If you allow three adults to live in a two-bedroom apartment, you had better let a couple with a child live in the same type of unit, or you are leaving yourself open to charges that you are illegally discriminating.

Clause 4.   Term of the Tenancy

This clause sets out the key difference between a lease and a rental agreement: how long a rent-paying tenant is entitled to stay.

Section A, above, discusses the pros and cons of leases and rental agreements, including notice requirements to change or end a tenancy.

a.   Lease Provision

The term of the rental will begin on _____,
200___ and end on _____, 200___. If Tenant vacates before the term ends, Tenant will be liable for the balance of the rent for the remainder of the term.

This lease provision sets a definite date for the beginning and the expiration of the lease and obligates both the landlord and the tenant for a specific term.

Most leases run for one year. This makes sense, because it allows you to raise the rent at reasonably frequent intervals if market conditions allow. Leases may be shorter (six months) or longer (24 months). This, of course, is up to you and the tenants. A long period—two, three or even five years—can be appropriate, for example, if you're renting out your own house because you're taking a two-year sabbatical or if you have agreed to allow a tenant to make major repairs or remodel your property at his expense.

How to Fill In Clause 4 (Lease):

In the blanks, fill in the starting date and the expiration date of the lease.

b.   Rental Agreement Provision

The rental will begin on _____,
200___, and continue on a month-to-month basis. Landlord may terminate the tenancy or modify the terms of this Agreement by giving the Tenant _____ days' written notice. Tenant may terminate the tenancy by giving the Landlord _____ days' written notice.

This rental agreement provides for a month-to-month tenancy and specifies how much written notice you must give a tenant to change or end a tenancy, and how much notice the tenant must provide you before moving out. (See Chapter 5, Section B, for a sample Tenant's Notice of Intent to Move Out form.)

How Many Tenants to Allow

Two kinds of laws affect the number of people who may live in a rental unit.

State and local health and safety codes typically set *maximum* limits on the number of tenants, based on the size of the unit and the number of bedrooms and bathrooms.

Even more important, the federal government has taken the lead in establishing *minimum* limits on the number of tenants, through passage of the Fair Housing Act (42 U.S. Code §§ 3601-3619, 3631) and by means of regulations from the Department of Housing and Urban Development (HUD). HUD generally considers a limit of two persons per bedroom a reasonable occupancy standard. Because the number of bedrooms is not the only factor—the size of the bedrooms and configuration of the rental unit are also considered —the federal test has become known as the "two per bedroom plus" standard. States and localities can set their own occupancy standards as long as they are more generous than the federal government's—that is, by allowing more people per rental unit.

The Fair Housing Act is designed primarily to disallow illegal discrimination against families with children, but it also allows you to establish your own "reasonable" restrictions on the number of people per rental unit—as long as your policy is truly tied to health and safety needs. In addition, you can adopt standards that are driven by a legitimate business reason or necessity, such as the capacities of the plumbing or electrical systems. Your personal preferences (such as a desire to reduce wear and tear by limiting the number of occupants or to ensure a quiet, uncrowded environment for upscale tenants), however, do not constitute a legitimate business reason. If your occupancy policy limits the number of tenants for any reason other than health, safety and legitimate business needs, you risk charges that you are discriminating against families.

Figuring out whether your occupancy policy is legal is not always a simple matter. Furthermore, laws on occupancy limits often change. For more information, call HUD's Fair Housing Information Clearinghouse at 800-767-7468, or check the HUD website at www.hud.gov. Check your local and state housing authority for other occupancy standards that may affect your rental property. Ask HUD for a referral if you're unsure what state or local agency to call.

How to Fill In Clause 4 (Rental Agreement):

In the first blank, fill in the date the tenancy will begin.

In the next two blanks, fill in the amount of written notice you'll need to give tenants to end or change a tenancy and the amount of notice tenants must provide to end a tenancy. In most cases, to comply with the law of your state, this will be 30 days for both landlord and tenant in a month-to-month tenancy. (See the "Notice Required to Change or Terminate a Month-to-Month Tenancy" chart in Appendix 1 for a list of each state's notice requirements.)

Possible Modifications to Clause 4 (Rental Agreement):

This rental agreement is month to month, although you can change it to a different interval as long as you don't go below the minimum notice period required by your state's law. If you do, be aware that notice requirements to change or end a tenancy may also need to differ from those required for standard month-to-month rental agreements, since state law often requires that all key notice periods be the same.

Your right to terminate or change the terms of a tenancy, even one from month to month, can be limited by a rent control ordinance. Check local rules for details.

Clause 5.   Payment of Rent

Regular monthly rent.
Tenant will pay to Landlord a monthly rent of $_____, payable in advance on the first day of each month, except when that day falls on a weekend or legal holiday, in which case rent is due on the next business day. Rent will be paid in the following manner, unless Landlord designates otherwise:

Delivery of payment.
Rent will be paid:
☐ by mail, to _____
☐ in person, at _____

Form of payment.
Landlord will accept payment in these forms:
☐ personal check made payable to _____
☐ cashier's check made payable to _____
☐ credit card
☐ money order
☐ cash

Prorated first month's rent.
For the period from Tenant's move-in date, _____, 200__, through the end of the month, Tenant will pay to Landlord the prorated monthly rent of $_____. This amount will be paid on or before the date the Tenant moves in.

This clause provides details on the amount of rent and when, where and how it's paid. It requires the tenant to pay rent monthly on the first day of the month, unless the first day falls on a weekend or a legal holiday, in which case rent is due on the next business day. (Extending the rent due date for holidays is legally required in some states and is a general rule in most.)

How to Fill In Clause 5:

Regular monthly rent. In the first blank, state the amount of monthly rent. Unless your premises are subject to a local rent control ordinance, you can legally charge as much rent as you want (or, more practically speaking, as much as a tenant will pay).

Delivery of payment. Next, specify to whom and where the rent is to be paid—by mail (most common) or in person (if so, specify the address, such as your office or to your manager at the rental unit).

Form of payment. Note all the forms of payment you'll accept, such as personal check and money order.

⚠️ ***Don't accept cash unless you have no choice.***

You face an increased risk of robbery if word gets out that you are taking in large amounts of cash once or twice a month. And if you accept cash knowing that the tenant earned it from an illegal act such as drug dealing, the government could seize the money from you under federal and state forfeiture laws. For both these reasons, we recommend that you insist that rent be paid by check, money order or credit card. If you do accept cash, be sure to provide a written, dated receipt stating the tenant's name and the amount of rent paid. Such a receipt is required by law in a few states, and it's a good idea everywhere.

Prorated first month's rent. If the tenant moves in before the regular rental period—let's say in the middle of the month, and you want rent due on the first of every month—you can specify the prorated amount due for the first partial month. To figure out prorated rent, divide the monthly rent by 30 days and multiply by the number of days in the first rental period. That will avoid confusion about what you expect to be paid. Enter the move-in date, such as "June 21, 200X," and the amount of prorated monthly rent.

EXAMPLE: Meg rents an apartment for $900 per month, with rent due on the first of the month. She moves in on June 21, so she should pay ten days' prorated rent of $300 when she moves in. ($900/30=$30 x 10 days=$300.) The full $900 July rent is due on July 1.

If the tenant is moving in on the first of the month, or the same day rent is due, write in "N/A" or "Not Applicable" in the section on prorated rent, or delete this section of the clause.

Possible Modifications to Clause 5:

Here are a few common ways to modify Clause 5:

Rent due date. You can establish a rent due date different from the first of the month, such as the day of the month on which the tenant moves in. For example, if the tenant moved in on July 10, rent would be due on that date, a system which of course saves the trouble of prorating the first month's rent.

Frequency of rent payments. You are not legally required to have your tenant pay rent on a monthly basis. You can modify the clause and require that the rent be paid twice a month, each week or by whatever schedule suits you.

Rent Control

Communities in only five states—California, the District of Columbia, Maryland, New Jersey and New York—have laws that limit the amount of rent landlords may charge and how and when rent may be increased. Typically, only a few cities or counties in each of these states have enacted local rent control ordinances (also called rent stabilization, maximum rent regulation or a similar term), but often these are some of the state's largest cities—for example, San Francisco, Los Angeles, New York City and Newark all have some form of rent control.

Rent control laws commonly regulate much more than rent. For example, owners of rent-controlled properties must often follow specific "just cause" eviction procedures. And local rent control ordinances may require that your lease or rental agreement include certain information —for example, the address of the local rent control board.

If you own rental property in a city that has rent control, you should always have a current copy of the ordinance and any regulations interpreting it. Check with your local rent control board or city manager's or mayor's office for more information on rent control, and modify our forms accordingly.

- *Collecting deposits and potential problems with calling a deposit the "last month's rent": Clause 8, this chapter*
- *The value of highlighting your rent rules in a move-in letter to new tenants, and collecting the first month's rent: Chapter 4*
- *Tenant's obligations to pay rent when breaking a lease: Chapter 5*
- *Legal citations for state rent rules: Appendix 1*

Clause 6.   Late Charges

If Tenant fails to pay the rent in full before the end of the _____ day after it's due, Tenant will pay Landlord a late charge as follows: _____

_____.

Landlord does not waive the right to insist on payment of the rent in full on the date it is due.

It is your legal right to charge a late fee if rent is not paid on time. This clause spells out details of your policy on late fees. A few states have statutes that put precise limits on the amount of late fees or when they can be collected. (See the Late Fees column in the "State Rent Rules" table in Appendix 1 before completing this clause.)

Some rent control ordinances also regulate late fees. If you own rental units in a municipality with rent control, check the ordinances carefully.

But even if your state doesn't have specific rules restricting late fees, you are still bound by general legal principles (often expressed in court decisions) that prohibit unreasonably high fees. Unless your state imposes more specific statutory rules on late fees, you should be on safe ground if you adhere to these principles:

- The total late charge should not exceed 4%-5% of the rent.
- If the late fee increases each day the rent is late, it should be moderate and have an

upper limit. A late charge that increases without a maximum could be considered interest charged at an illegal ("usurious") rate. Although state usury laws don't directly apply to late charges, judges often use these laws as one guideline in judging whether a particular provision is reasonable. Most states set their maximum interest rate at about 10% to 12%. A late charge that would generally be acceptable for a $1,000 per month rent would be a charge of $10 if rent is not paid by the end of the second business day after it is due, plus $5 for each additional day, up to a maximum of 5% of the monthly rental amount.

Don't try to disguise excessive late charges by giving a "discount" for early payment.

One landlord we know concluded that he couldn't get away with charging a $100 late charge on a $850 rent payment, so, instead, he designed a rental agreement calling for a rent of $950 with a $100 discount if the rent was not more than three days late. Ingenious as this ploy sounds, it is unlikely to stand up in court in many states, unless the discount for timely payment is modest. Giving a relatively large discount is in effect the same as charging an excessive late fee, and a judge is likely to see it as such.

How to Fill In Clause 6:

In the first blank, specify if you will allow a grace period before you charge a late fee. You don't have to give a grace period, but many landlords don't charge a late fee until the rent is two or three days late. If you don't allow any grace period, simply cross out the first blank and the word "after," so that the first line reads "If Tenant fails to pay the rent in full before the end of the day it's due … ."

Next, fill in details on your late rent fee, such as the daily charge and any maximum fee.

Possible Modifications to Clause 6:

If you decide not to charge a late fee (something we consider highly unwise), you may simply delete this clause, or write the words "N/A" or "Not Applicable" on it.

Clause 7. Returned Check and Other Bank Charges

If any check offered by Tenant to Landlord in payment of rent or any other amount due under this Agreement is returned for lack of sufficient funds, a "stop payment" or any other reason, Tenant will pay Landlord a returned check charge of $_____.

As with late charges, any bounced-check charges you require must be reasonable. Generally, you should charge no more than the amount your bank charges you for a returned check, probably $10 to $20 per returned item, plus a few dollars for your trouble. Check with your state consumer protection agency for any restrictions on bounced-check charges. For a list of state consumer protection agencies, go to the site maintained by the Federal Consumer Information Center at www.pueblo.gsa.gov/crh/state.htm.

Don't tolerate repeated bad checks.
If a tenant habitually pays rent late or gives you bad checks, give written notice demanding that the tenant pay the rent or move within a few days. How long the tenant is allowed to stay depends on state law; in most places, it's about three to fifteen days. In most instances, the tenant who receives this kind of "pay rent or quit" notice pays up and reforms his ways, and that's the end of it. But, if the tenant doesn't pay the rent (or move), you can file an eviction lawsuit. An alternative is to serve the tenant with a 30-day notice to change Clause 5 of the lease or rental agreement to require payment with a money order or a verified credit card transaction.

How to Fill In Clause 7:

In the blank, fill in the amount of the returned check charge. If you won't accept checks, fill in "N/A" or "Not Applicable."

Clause 8. Security Deposit

On signing this Agreement, Tenant will pay to Landlord the sum of $_____ as a security deposit. Tenant may not, without Landlord's prior written consent, apply this security deposit to the last month's rent or to any other sum due under this Agreement. Within _____ after Tenant has vacated the premises, returned keys and provided Landlord with a forwarding address, Landlord will return the deposit in full or give Tenant an itemized written statement of the reasons for, and the dollar amount of, any of the security deposit retained by Landlord, along with a check for any deposit balance.

Most landlords quite sensibly ask for a security deposit before entrusting hundreds of thousands of dollars worth of real estate to a tenant. But it's easy to get into legal trouble over deposits, because they are strictly regulated by state law and, sometimes, also by city ordinance. The law of most states dictates how large a deposit you can require, how you can use it, when you must return it and more. Several states require you to put deposits in a separate account and pay interest on them.

The use and return of security deposits is a frequent source of disputes between landlords and tenants. To avoid confusion and legal hassles, this clause is clear on the subject, including:

- the dollar amount of the deposit
- the fact that the deposit may not be used for the last month's rent without your prior approval, and
- when the deposit will be returned, along with an itemized statement of deductions.

This section discusses the basic information you need to complete Clause 8. Check the tables on security deposit rules in Appendix 1 for specific details that apply to your situation:

- State Security Deposit Rules
- States That Require Landlords to Maintain a Separate Account for Security Deposits
- States That Require Landlords to Pay Interest on Deposits

If, after reviewing these tables, you have any questions of what's allowed in your state, you should get a current copy of your state's security deposit statute or an up-to-date summary from a landlords' association. In addition, be sure to check local ordinances in all areas where you own property. Cities, particularly those with rent control, may add additional rules on security deposits, such as a limit on the amount you can charge or a requirement that you pay interest on deposits.

Basic State Rules on Security Deposits

All states allow you to collect a security deposit when a tenant moves in and hold it until the tenant leaves. The general purpose of a security deposit is to assure that a tenant pays the rent when it is due and keeps the rental unit in good condition. Rent you collect in advance for the first month is not typically considered part of the security deposit.

State laws typically control the amount you can charge and how and when you must return security deposits:

- Many states limit the amount you can collect as a deposit to a maximum of one or two months' rent. Sometimes, the limit in a particular state is higher for furnished units.
- Several states require landlords to pay tenants interest on security deposits, and establish detailed requirements as to the interest rate

that must be paid. Some states require you to put deposits in a separate account, sometimes called a "trust" account, rather than mixing the funds with your personal or business accounts. In most states, however, you don't have to pay tenants interest on deposits or put them in a separate bank account. In other words, you can simply put the money in your pocket or bank account and use it, as long as you have it available when the tenant moves out.

- When a tenant moves out, you will have a set amount of time (usually from 14 to 30 days, depending on the state) to either return the tenant's entire deposit or provide an itemized statement of deductions and refund any deposit balance.
- You can generally withhold all or part of the deposit to pay for:
  - Unpaid rent.
  - Repairing damage to the premises (except for "ordinary wear and tear") caused by the tenant, a family member or a guest.
  - Cleaning necessary to restore the rental unit to its condition at the beginning of the tenancy (over and above "ordinary wear and tear").
  - Restoring or replacing rental unit property taken by the tenant. States typically also allow you to use a deposit to cover the tenant's other obligations under the lease or rental agreement, which may include payment of utility charges.
- The laws of many states set heavy penalties for violation of security deposit statutes. (See Chapter 5, Section D.)

Don't Charge Nonrefundable Deposits

State laws are often muddled on the subject of whether charging nonrefundable deposits and fees is legal. Some specifically allow landlords to collect a fee that is not refundable—such as for pets, cleaning or redecorating—as long as this is clearly stated in the lease or rental agreement. In addition, most states allow landlords to charge propsective tenants a nonrefundable fee for the cost of a credit report and related screening fees (discussed in Chapter 3, Section D).

But many states—and this is clearly the trend—have enacted security deposit statutes that specifically prohibit nonrefundable fees such as a fixed fee for cleaning drapes or carpets or for painting; all such fees are legally considered security deposits, no matter what they are labeled in the lease or rental agreement, and must be refundable. It is also illegal in many states to make the return of deposits contingent upon a tenant staying for a minimum period of time.

Generally, it's best to avoid the legal uncertainties and not try to collect any nonrefundable fees from tenants. In addition, most landlords have found that making all deposits refundable avoids many time-consuming arguments and even lawsuits with tenants. We believe it's much simpler just to consider the expenses these fees cover as part of your overhead and figure them into the rent, raising it, if necessary.

If you have a specific concern about a particular tenant—for example, you're afraid a tenant's pet will damage the carpets or furniture—just ask for a higher security deposit (but do check your state's maximum). That way, you're covered if the pet causes damage, and, if it doesn't, the tenant won't have to shell out unnecessarily.

If, despite our advice, you want to charge a nonrefundable fee, check your state's law to find what (if any) kinds of nonrefundable fees are allowed. Then, make sure your lease or rental agreement is clear on the subject.

How Much Deposit Should You Charge?

Normally, the best advice is to charge as much as the market will bear, within any legal limits. The more the tenant has at stake, the better the chance your property will be respected. And, the larger the deposit, the more financial protection you will have if a tenant leaves owing you rent.

The market, however, often keeps the practical limit on deposits lower than the maximum allowed by law. Your common sense and your business sense need to work together in setting security deposits. Here are a number of considerations to keep in mind:

- **Charge the full limit in high-risk situations:** where there's a lot of tenant turnover, if the tenant has a pet and you're concerned about damage or if the tenant's credit is shaky and you're worried about unpaid rent.

- **Consider the psychological advantage of a higher rent rather than a high deposit.** Many tenants would rather pay a slightly higher rent than an enormous deposit. Also, many acceptable, solvent tenants have a hard time coming up with several months' rent, especially if they are still in a rental unit and are awaiting the return of a previous security deposit.

- **Charge a bigger deposit for single-family homes.** Unlike multi-unit residences, where close-by neighbors or a manager can spot, report and quickly stop any destruction of the premises, the single-family home is somewhat of an island. The condition of the interior and even the exterior may be hard to assess, unless you live close by or can frequently check the condition of a single-family rental. And, of course, the cost of repairing damage to a house is likely to be higher than for an apartment.

- **Gain a marketing advantage by allowing a deposit to be paid in installments.** If rentals are plentiful in your area, with comparable units renting at about the same price, you might gain a competitive edge by allowing

20180209

tenants to pay the deposit in several installments, rather than one lump sum.

Require renter's insurance as an alternative to a high security deposit.
If you're worried about damage but don't think you can raise the deposit any higher, require renter's insurance. You can give your property an extra measure of protection by insisting that the tenant purchase renter's insurance, which may cover damage done by the tenant or guests. (See sidebar, "Renter's Insurance," under Clause 11.)

Last Month's Rent

It's a common—but often unwise—practice to collect a sum of money called "last month's rent" from a tenant who's moving in. Landlords tend to treat this money as just another security deposit, and use it to cover not only the last month's rent but also other expenses such as repairs or cleaning.

Problems can arise because some states restrict the use of money labeled as the "last month's rent" to its stated purpose: the rent for the tenant's last month of occupancy. If you use any of it to repair damage by the former tenant, you're violating the law. Also, using the "last month's rent" for cleaning and repairs may lead to a dispute with a tenant who feels that the last month's rent is taken care of and resents having to pay all or part of it. You would be better off if the tenant paid the last month's rent when it came due, leaving the entire security deposit available to cover cleaning and repairs.

Avoiding the term "last month's rent" also keeps things simpler if you raise the rent, but not the deposit, before the tenant's last month of occupancy. The problem arises when rent for the tenant's last month becomes due. Has the tenant already paid in full, or does he owe more because the monthly rent is now higher? Legally, there is often no clear

answer. In practice, it's a hassle you are best to avoid by not labeling any part of the security deposit "last month's rent."

Clause 8 of the form agreements makes it clear that the tenant may not apply the security deposit to the last month's rent.

How to Fill In Clause 8:

Once you decide how much security deposit you can charge (see "State Security Deposit Rules" in Appendix 1), fill in the amount in the first blank. Unless there's a lower limit, we suggest about two months as your rent deposit, assuming your potential tenants can afford that much. (See "How Much Deposit Should You Charge?," above.) In no case is it wise to charge much less than one month's rent.

Next, fill in the time period when you will return the deposit, also using the table "State Security Deposit Rules" in Appendix 1. If there is no statutory deadline for returning the deposit, we recommend 14 to 21 days as a reasonable time to return a tenant's deposit. Establishing a fairly short period (even if the law of your state allows more time) will discourage anxious tenants from repeatedly bugging you or your manager for their deposit refund. (See the discussion of returning security deposits.)

Possible Modifications to Clause 8:

The laws of several states require you to give tenants written information on various aspects of the security deposit, including where the security deposit is being held, interest payments and the terms of and conditions under which the security deposit may be withheld. The chart below, "State-Mandated Additions to Security Deposit Clause," lists specific clauses you should add to Clause 8. (See sidebar, "How to Prepare Attachment Pages," at the beginning of this section.)

State-Mandated Additions to Security Deposit Clause

State	Add this language to the security deposit clause:
Alaska	"Landlord will retain only that portion of Tenant's security deposit necessary to pay accrued rent or compensate Landlord for damages suffered by reason of Tenant's failure to maintain the dwelling unit."
Florida	"The security deposit will be held in [a separate or Landlord's] [interest-bearing or non-interest bearing] account at: [name and address of depository].
	"Interest will be paid on this account as follows: [rate, time of payments].
	"A copy of Florida Statutes § 83.49(3), explaining how and when the security deposit will be returned, is attached as required by law." [*A copy for you to attach is included in Appendix 1 of this book.*]
Georgia	"The security deposit will be held in escrow account no. _____ at: [name and address of depository]."
Kentucky	"The security deposit will be held in account no. _____ at: [name and address of depository]."
Maryland	"Tenant has the right to receive from Landlord a written list of all existing damages if Tenant requests by certified mail within 15 days of Tenant's occupancy."
Michigan	"The security deposit will be held in an account at: [name and address of depository]."
	You must also add the following paragraph in 12-point boldface type or type that is at least four points larger than the body of the agreement:
	"To the Tenant: You must notify your landlord in writing within 4 days after you move of a forwarding address where you can be reached and where you will receive mail; otherwise your landlord shall be relieved of sending you an itemized list of damages and the penalties adherent to that failure."
North Carolina	"The security deposit will be held in account no. _____ at: [name and address of depository] or by [name and address of insurance company providing bond for security deposit]."
Tennessee	"The security deposit will be held at: [name and address of depository]."
Washington	"The security deposit will be held in an account at: [name and address of depository]."
	"Landlord may withhold only that portion of the security deposit necessary to (1) remedy any default in the payment of rent, (2) repair damage to the premises, except ordinary wear and tear, caused by Tenant and (3) clean the premises if necessary."

Even if it's not required, you may want to provide additional details on security deposits in your lease or rental agreement. Here are optional clauses you may add to the end of Clause 8.

The security deposit will be held at:_____
_____ (name and address of financial institution) _____ .
Landlord will pay Tenant interest on all security deposits as follows: _____ (interest terms) _____ .

Landlord may withhold only that portion of Tenant's security deposit necessary to: (1) remedy any default by Tenant in the payment of rent; (2) repair damage to the premises, except for ordinary wear and tear caused by Tenant; (3) clean the premises if necessary; and (4) compensate Landlord for any other losses as allowed by state law.

Clause 9.   Utilities

Tenant will pay all utility charges, except for the following, which will be paid by Landlord:_____
_____

This clause helps prevent misunderstandings as to who's responsible for paying utilities. Normally, landlords pay for garbage (and sometimes water, if there is a yard) to help make sure that the premises are well maintained. Tenants usually pay for other services, such as phone, gas, electricity and cable TV.

How to Fill In Clause 9:

In the blank, fill in the utilities you—not the tenants—will be responsible for paying. If you will not be paying for any utilities, simply write in "N/A" or "Not Applicable."

Disclose Shared Utility Arrangements

If there are not separate gas and electric meters for each unit, or a tenant's meter serves any areas outside his unit (such as a water heater used in common with other tenants or even a light bulb not under the tenant's control in a common area), you should disclose this in your lease or rental agreement. Simply add details to Clause 9, preparing an attachment page if necessary. This type of disclosure is required by law in some states, and is only fair in any case. The best solution is to put in a separate meter for the areas served outside the tenant's unit. If you don't do that, you should:

- pay for the utilities for the tenant's meter yourself by placing that utility in your name
- reduce the tenant's rent to compensate for payment of utility usage outside of her unit (this will probably cost you more in the long run than if you either added a new meter or simply paid for the utilities yourself), or
- sign a separate written agreement with the tenant, under which the tenant specifically agrees to pay for others' utilities, too.

Clause 10. Assignment and Subletting

Tenant will not sublet any part of the premises or assign this Agreement without the prior written consent of Landlord.

Clause 10 is an anti-subletting clause, breach of which is grounds for eviction. It prevents a tenant from subleasing during a vacation or renting out a room to someone unless you specifically agree.

Clause 10 is also designed to prevent assignments, a legal term that means your tenant transfers her tenancy to someone else. Practically, you need this clause to prevent your tenant from leaving in the middle of the month or lease term and moving in a replacement—maybe someone you wouldn't choose to rent to—without your consent.

By including Clause 10 in your lease or rental agreement, you have the option not to accept the person your tenant proposes to take over the lease. Under the law of most states, however, you should realize that if a tenant who wishes to leave early provides you with another suitable tenant, you can't both unreasonably refuse to rent to this person and hold the tenant financially liable for breaking the lease. Typically, state law requires that you must try to re-rent the property reasonably quickly and subtract any rent you receive from the amount the original tenant owed you for the remainder of the agreed-upon rental period. Lawyers call this the mitigation-of-damages rule, a bit of legalese it's valuable to know.

How to Fill In Clause 10:

You don't need to add anything to this clause in most situations. There may be local laws, however, that do apply.

For a related discussion of subleases, assignments and the landlord's duty to mitigate damages, see Chapter 5, Section C. Also, Chapter 8 of Every Landlord's Legal Guide, *by Marcia Stewart, Ralph Warner & Janet Portman (Nolo), covers these topics in detail.*

Common Terms

Tenant. Someone who has signed a lease or a rental agreement, or who has gained the status of a tenant because the landlord has accepted his presence on the property or has accepted rent from him.

Cotenants. Two or more tenants who rent the same property under the same lease or rental agreement, each 100% responsible for carrying out the agreement, including paying all the rent.

Subtenant. Someone who subleases (rents) all or part of the premises from a tenant and does not sign a lease or rental agreement with the landlord. A subtenant may either rent (sublet) an entire dwelling from a tenant who moves out temporarily—for example, for the summer—or rent one or more rooms from the tenant, who continues to live in the unit. The key to subtenant relationships is that the original tenant retains the primary relationship with the landlord and continues to exercise some control over the rental property, either by occupying part of the unit or by reserving the right to retake possession at a later date.

Assignment. The transfer by a tenant of all of his rights of tenancy to another tenant (the "assignee"). Unlike a subtenant, an assignee rents directly from the landlord.

Roommates. Two or more people, usually unrelated, living under the same roof and sharing rent and expenses. A roommate is usually a cotenant, but in some situations may be a subtenant.

Should You Allow a Sublet or Assignment?

As a general rule, your best bet when a tenant asks to sublease or assign is to simply insist that the tenancy terminate and a new one begin—with the proposed "subtenant" or "assignee" as the new tenant who signs a new lease or rental agreement. This gives you the most direct legal relationship with the substitute. There are a few situations, however, in which you may want to agree to a subtenancy or assignment.

You might, for example, want to accommodate—and keep—an exceptional, long-term tenant who has every intention of returning and whose judgment and integrity you have always trusted. If the proposed stand-in meets your normal tenant criteria, you may decide that it is worth the risk of a subtenancy or assignment in order to keep the original tenant.

Another good reason is a desire to have a sure source of funds in the background. This might come up if your original tenant is financially sound and trustworthy, but a proposed stand-in is less secure but acceptable in every other respect. By agreeing to a sublet or assignment, you have someone in the background (the original tenant) still responsible for the rent. The risk you incur by agreeing to set up a subtenancy or assignment and the hassle that comes with dealing with more than one person may be worth what you gain in keeping a sure and reliable source of funds on the hook.

Clause 11. Tenant's Maintenance Responsibilities

Tenant will: (1) keep the premises clean, sanitary and in good condition and, upon termination of the tenancy, return the premises to Landlord in a condition identical to that which existed when Tenant took occupancy, except for ordinary wear and tear; (2) immediately notify Landlord of any defects or dangerous conditions in and about the premises of which Tenant becomes aware; and (3) reimburse Landlord, on demand by Landlord, for the cost of any repairs to the premises damaged by Tenant or Tenant's guests or business invitees through misuse or neglect.

Tenant has examined the premises, including appliances, fixtures, carpets, drapes and paint, and has found them to be in good, safe and clean condition and repair, except as noted in the Landlord/Tenant Checklist.

Clause 11 makes the tenant responsible for keeping the rental premises clean and sanitary. This clause also makes it clear that if the tenant damages the premises—for example, by breaking a window or scratching hardwood floors—it's his responsibility to pay for the damage.

It is the law in some states (and a wise practice in all) to notify tenants in writing of procedures for making complaint and repair requests. Clause 11 requires the tenant to alert you to defective or dangerous conditions.

Before the tenant moves in, you and the tenant should inspect the rental unit and fill out the Landlord/Tenant Checklist in Chapter 4, describing what is in the unit and noting any problems. Doing so will help you avoid disputes over security deposit deductions when the tenant moves out.

How to Fill In Clause 11:

You do not need to add anything to this clause.

Avoid Problems by Adopting a Good Maintenance and Repair System

As a general rule, you are legally required to offer livable premises when a tenant originally rents an apartment or rental unit and to maintain the premises throughout the rental term. If rental property is not kept in good repair, the tenant may have the right to repair the problem and deduct the cost from the rent, withhold rent, sue for any injuries caused by defective conditions or move out without notice. Your best defense against rent withholding hassles and other disputes with tenants is to establish and communicate a clear, easy-to-follow procedure for tenants to ask for repairs and for you to document all complaints, respond quickly when complaints are made and schedule annual safety inspections. And, if you employ a manager or management company, make sure she or it fully accepts and implements your guidelines.

Follow these steps to avoid maintenance and repair problems with tenants:

1. Regularly look for dangerous conditions on the property and fix them promptly. Reduce risk exposure as much as possible—for example, by providing sufficient lighting in hallways, parking garages and other common areas, strong locks on doors and windows and safe stairs and handrails.

2. Scrupulously comply with all public health and safety codes. Your local building or housing authority, and health or fire department, can provide any information you need. Also, check state housing laws governing landlords' repair and maintenance responsibilities. (Appendix 1 includes citations for the major state laws affecting landlords. Check your statutes under headings such as Landlord Obligations to Maintain Premises.)

3. Clearly set out your and the tenant's responsibilities for repair and maintenance in your lease or rental agreement. (See Clauses 11, 12 and 13 of the agreements in this chapter.)

4. Use the written Landlord/Tenant Checklist form in Chapter 4 to check over the premises and fix any problems before new tenants move in.

5. Encourage tenants to immediately report plumbing, heating, weatherproofing or other defects and safety or security problems—whether in the tenant's unit or in common areas such as hallways and parking garages.

6. Handle repairs (especially urgent ones, such as a broken door lock or lack of heat in winter) as soon as possible. Notify the tenant by phone and follow up in writing if repairs will take more than 48 hours, excluding weekends. Keep the tenant informed—for example, if you have problems scheduling a plumber, let your tenant know with a phone call or a note. For nonurgent repairs, be sure to give the tenant proper notice as required by state law. (See Clause 15 for details on notice required to enter rental premises.)

7. Keep a written log of all tenant complaints, including those made orally. Record your immediate and any follow-up responses (and subsequent tenant communications) and details as to how and when the problem was fixed, including reasons for any delay.

8. Twice a year, give your tenants a checklist on which to report any potential safety hazards or problems that might have been overlooked—for example, low water pressure in the shower, peeling paint or noisy neighbors. This is also a good time to remind tenants of their repair and maintenance responsibilities. Respond promptly and in writing to all repair requests, keeping copies in your file.

9. Once a year, inspect all rental units for safety and maintenance problems, using the Landlord/Tenant Checklist as a guide. Make sure smoke detectors, heating and plumbing systems and major appliances are in fact safe and in good working order. (Keep copies of the filled-in checklist in your file.)

10. Get a good liability insurance policy to cover injuries or losses suffered by others as the result of defective conditions on the property and lawyers' bills for defending personal injury suits.

Renter's Insurance

It is becoming increasingly popular, especially in high-end rentals, to require tenants to obtain renter's insurance. This insurance covers losses to the tenant's belongings as a result of fire or theft. Often called a "Tenant's Package Policy," renter's insurance also covers the tenant if his negligence causes injury to other people or property damage (to his property or to yours). Besides protecting the tenant from personal liability, renter's insurance benefits you, too: If damage caused by the tenant could be covered by either his insurance policy or yours—for example, the tenant accidentally starts a fire when he leaves the stove on—a claim made on the tenant's policy will affect his premiums, not yours.

If you decide to require insurance, insert a clause like the following at the end of your lease or rental agreement, under Clause 22, Additional Provisions. This will help assure that the tenant purchases and maintains a renter's insurance policy throughout his tenancy.

Renter's Insurance

Within ten days of the signing of this Agreement, Tenant will obtain renter's insurance and provide proof of purchase to Landlord. Tenant further agrees to maintain the policy throughout the duration of the tenancy, and to furnish proof of insurance on a ☐ yearly ☐ semi-annual basis.

Several times in this book, we recommend Every Landlord's Legal Guide *by Marcia Stewart, Ralph Warner & Janet Portman (Nolo). It is especially useful for its detailed discussion of landlords' and tenants' rights and responsibilities for repair and maintenance under state and local laws and judicial decisions. It provides practical advice on how to stay on top of repair and maintenance needs and minimize financial losses and legal problems with tenants. It discusses tenants' rights if you do not meet your legal responsibilities and the pros and cons of delegating repairs and maintenance to the tenant. Every Landlord's Legal Guide also includes chapters on landlords' liability for tenant injuries from defective housing conditions, such as a broken step or defective wiring; liability for environmental hazards such as asbestos and lead; and responsibility to provide secure premises and protect tenants from assault or criminal activities, such as drug dealing.*

Clause 12. Repairs and Alterations by Tenant

a. Except as provided by law or as authorized by the prior written consent of Landlord, Tenant will not make any repairs or alterations to the premises, including nailing holes in the walls or painting the rental unit.

b. Tenant will not, without Landlord's prior written consent, alter, re-key or install any locks to the premises or install or alter any burglar alarm system. Tenant will provide Landlord with a key or keys capable of unlocking all such re-keyed or new locks as well as instructions on how to disarm any altered or new burglar alarm system.

Clause 12 makes it clear that the tenant may not make alterations and repairs without your consent, including painting or nailing holes in the walls.

And, to make sure you can take advantage of your legal right of entry in an emergency situation, Clause 12 specifically forbids the tenant from re-keying the locks or installing a burglar alarm system without your consent. If you do grant permission, make sure your tenant gives you duplicate keys or the name and phone number of the alarm company or instructions on how to disarm the alarm system so that you can enter in case of emergency.

The "except as provided by law" language in Clause 12 is a reference to the fact that, in certain situations and in certain states, tenants have a narrowly defined right to alter or repair the premises, regardless of what you've said in the lease or rental agreement. Examples include:

- **Alterations by a disabled person, such as lowering countertops for a wheelchair-bound tenant**. Under the federal Fair Housing Act, a disabled person may modify her living space to the extent necessary to make the space safe and comfortable, as long as the modifications will not make the unit unacceptable to the next tenant, or if the disabled tenant agrees to undo the modification when she leaves. (42 U.S.C. § 3604(f)(3)(A).)

- **Use of the "repair and deduct" procedure.** In most states, tenants have the right to repair defects or damage that make the premises uninhabitable or substantially interfere with the tenant's safe use or enjoyment of the premises. Usually, the tenant must first notify you of the problem and give you a reasonable amount of time to fix it.

- **Installation of satellite dishes and antennas.** Federal law gives tenants limited rights to install wireless antennas and small satellite dishes. (47 C.F.R. § 1.4000.)

- **Specific alterations allowed by state statutes.** Some states allow tenants to install energy conservation measures (like removable interior storm windows) or burglary prevention devices without the landlord's prior consent. Check your state statutes or call your local rental property association for more information on these types of laws.

How to Fill In Clause 12:

If you do not want the tenant to make any repairs without your permission, you do not need to add anything to this clause.

You may, however, want to go further and specifically prohibit certain repairs or alterations by adding details in Clause 22 (Additional Provisions). For example, you may want to make it clear that any "fixtures"—a legal term that describes any addition that is attached to the structure, such as bolted-in bookcases or built-in dishwashers—are your property and may not be removed by the tenant without your permission. See sidebar, "How

to Prepare Attachment Pages," at the beginning of this section for advice on adding language to a clause.

If you do authorize the tenant to make any repairs, provide enough detail (on an attachment page) so that the tenant knows exactly what is expected, how much repairs can cost and who will pay. For example, if you decide to allow the tenant to take over the repair of any broken windows, routine plumbing jobs or landscaping, give specific descriptions and limits to the tasks.

⚠ **Do not delegate to a tenant your responsibility for major maintenance of essential services.**

The duty to repair and maintain heating, plumbing and electrical and structural systems (the roof, for example) is yours. Absent unusual circumstances, and even then only after carefully checking state law, it's a mistake to try to delegate this responsibility to the tenant. Many courts have held that landlords cannot delegate to a tenant the responsibility for keeping the premises fit for habitation, fearing that the tenant will rarely be in the position, either practically or financially, to do the kinds of repairs that are often needed to bring a structure up to par.

Clause 13. Violating Laws and Causing Disturbances

Tenant is entitled to quiet enjoyment of the premises. Tenant and guests or invitees will not use the premises or adjacent areas in such a way as to: (1) violate any law or ordinance, including laws prohibiting the use, possession or sale of illegal drugs; (2) commit waste (severe property damage); or (3) create a nuisance by annoying, disturbing, inconveniencing or interfering with the quiet enjoyment and peace and quiet of any other tenant or nearby resident.

This type of clause is found in most form leases and rental agreements. Although it contains some legal jargon, it's probably best to leave it as is, since courts have much experience in working with these terms. As courts define it, the "covenant of quiet enjoyment" amounts to an implied promise that you will not act (or fail to act) in a way that interferes with or destroys the ability of the tenant to use the rented premises.

Examples of violations of the covenant of quiet enjoyment include:

- allowing garbage to pile up
- tolerating a major rodent infestation, or
- failing to control a tenant whose constant loud music makes it impossible for other tenants to sleep.

If you want more specific rules—for example, no loud music played after midnight—add them to Clause 18: Rules and Regulations, or to Clause 22: Additional Provisions.

How to Fill In Clause 13:

You do not need to add anything to this clause.

Waste and Nuisance: What Are They?

In legalese, committing **waste** means causing severe damage to real estate, including a house or an apartment unit—damage that goes way beyond ordinary wear and tear. Punching holes in walls, pulling out sinks and fixtures and knocking down doors are examples of waste.

Nuisance means behavior that prevents neighbors from fully enjoying the use of their homes. Continuous loud noise and foul odors are examples of legal nuisances that may disturb nearby neighbors. So, too, are selling drugs or engaging in other illegal activities that greatly disturb neighbors.

How to Prevent Illegal Tenant Activity

There are several practical steps you can take both to avoid trouble among your tenants and, in the event that hostilities do erupt, to limit your exposure to lawsuits:

- Screen tenants carefully and choose tenants who are likely to be law-abiding and peaceful citizens. (Chapter 3 recommends a comprehensive system for screening prospective tenants, including checking out references from past landlords and employers.)
- Establish a system to respond to tenants' complaints and concerns about other tenants, especially those involving drug dealing on the rental property.
- Make it clear that you will not tolerate tenants' disruptive behavior. An explicit lease or rental agreement provision such as Clause 13 prohibiting drug dealing and illegal activity is the most effective way to make this point. If a tenant does cause trouble, act swiftly. Some situations, such as drug dealing, call for prompt efforts to evict the troublemaker. Your failure to evict drug-dealing tenants can result in lawsuits from tenants injured or annoyed by drug dealers, and local, state or federal authorities may choose to levy stiff fines for allowing the illegal activity to continue. In extreme cases, you may actually lose your property to the government under public nuisance abatement laws and forfeiture laws.

Clause 14. Pets

No animal, bird or other pet will be kept on the premises, even temporarily, except properly trained dogs needed by blind, deaf or disabled persons and _____

_____

under the following conditions:_____

_____.

This clause is designed to prevent tenants from keeping pets without your written permission. This is not necessarily to say that you will want to apply a flat "no-pets" rule. (Many landlords, in fact, report that pet-owning tenants are more appreciative, stable and responsible than the norm.) But it does provide you with a legal mechanism designed to keep your premises from being waist-deep in Irish wolfhounds. Without this sort of provision, particularly if you use a longer-term lease that can't be terminated early save for a clear violation of one of its provisions, there's little to prevent your tenant from keeping dangerous or nonhousebroken pets on your property, except for city ordinances prohibiting tigers and the like.

You have the right to prohibit all pets, or to restrict the types of pets you allow, with the exception of trained dogs used by blind, deaf or physically or mentally disabled people.

How to Fill in Clause 14:

If you do not allow pets, put the word "None" in the blanks.

If you allow pets, be sure to identify the type and number of pets in the first blank—for example, "one cat" or "one dog under 20 pounds." It's also wise to spell out your pet rules in the second blank—or in an attachment; for example, you may want to specify that the tenants will keep the yard free of all animal waste and that pets must be well-trained and nonthreatening to other tenants or other people on or near the rental premises. (Your Rules and Regulations may be another place to do this. See Clause 18.)

Renting to Pet Owners

Project Open Door, an ambitious program of the San Francisco Society for the Prevention of Cruelty to Animals (SPCA), seeks to show landlords how to make renting to pet-owning tenants a satisfying and profitable experience. The SPCA offers landlords:

- checklists to help screen pet-owning tenants
- pet policies to add to standard leases and rental agreements, and
- free mediation if landlords and tenants have pet-related problems after moving in.

For more information, contact the San Francisco SPCA at 2500 16th St., San Francisco, CA 94103, 415-554-3000, or check its website at www.sfspca.org/opendoor. Also, see *Dog Law*, by Mary Randolph (Nolo), for more information on renting to pet owners.

Should You Require a Separate Security Deposit for Pets?

Some landlords allow pets but require the tenant to pay a separate deposit to cover any damages caused by the pet. The laws of a few states specifically allow separate, nonrefundable pet deposits. In others, charging a designated pet deposit is legal only if the total amount you charge for deposits does not exceed the state maximum for all deposits. (See Clause 8 for details on security deposits.)

Even where allowed, separate pet deposits can often be a bad idea, because they limit how you can use that part of the security deposit. For example, if the pet is well behaved but the tenant trashes your unit, you can't use the pet portion of the deposit to clean up after the human. If you want to protect your property from damage done by a pet, you are probably better off charging a slightly higher rent or security deposit to start with (assuming you are not restricted by rent control or the upper security deposit limits).

⚠️ *It is illegal to charge an extra pet deposit for people with trained guide dogs, signal dogs or service dogs.*

Clause 15. Landlord's Right to Access

Landlord or Landlord's agents may enter the premises in the event of an emergency, to make repairs or improvements or to show the premises to prospective buyers or tenants. Landlord may also enter the premises to conduct an annual inspection to check for safety or maintenance problems. Except in cases of emergency, Tenant's abandonment of the premises, court order or where it is impractical to do so, Landlord shall give Tenant _____ notice before entering.

The tenant's duty to pay rent is typically conditioned on your having fulfilled your legal responsibility to properly repair and maintain the premises. This means that, of necessity, you have a legal responsibility to keep fairly close tabs on the condition of the property. For this reason, and because it makes good sense to allow landlords reasonable access to their property, nearly every state clearly recognizes the right of a landlord to legally enter rented premises while a tenant is still in residence under certain broad circumstances, such as to deal with an emergency and when the tenant gives permission.

About half the states have access laws specifying the circumstances under which landlords may legally enter rented premises. Most access laws allow landlords to enter rental units to make repairs and inspect the property and to show property to prospective tenants. (See sidebar, "General Rules of Entry," below.) State access laws typically specify the amount of notice required for such entry—usually 24 hours (unless it is impractical to do so—for example, in cases of emergency). A few states simply require the landlord to provide "reasonable" notice, often presumed to be 24 hours.

Clause 15 makes it clear to the tenant that you have a legal right of access to the property to make repairs or to show the premises for sale or rental, provided you give the tenant reasonable notice. (The table "State Laws on Landlord's Access to Rental Property" in Appendix 1 provides details on a landlord's right to entry and notice requirements.)

How to Fill In Clause 15:

In the blank, indicate the amount of notice you will provide the tenant before entering—at least the minimum required in your state. If your state law simply requires "reasonable" notice or has no notice requirement, we suggest you provide at least 24 hours' notice.

General Rules of Entry

Here are the general circumstances under which landlords may legally enter rented premises. Except in cases of emergency, or where it is impractical to do so, you generally must enter only at reasonable times, and you must give at least the amount and type of notice required in your state.

Emergency. In all states, you can enter rental property to respond to a true emergency —such as a gas leak.

To make repairs or inspect the property. By law, many states allow you and your repairperson to enter the tenant's home to make necessary or agreed-upon repairs, decorations, alterations or improvements and to supply necessary or agreed-upon services—for example, when you need to fix a broken oven.

To show property. Most states with access laws allow a landlord to enter rented property to show it to prospective tenants toward the end of the tenancy or to prospective purchasers if the landlord wishes to sell the property. (See Chapter 3, Section B for advice on renting property that's still occupied.)

With the permission of the tenant. You can always enter rental property, even without notice, if the tenant agrees.

Entry after the tenant has moved out. To state the obvious, you may enter the premises after the tenant has completely moved out— regardless of whether the tenant left voluntarily after giving back the key or involuntarily as a result of an eviction lawsuit. In addition, if you believe the tenant has abandoned the property—that is, skipped out without giving any notice or returning the key—you may legally enter.

Clause 16. Extended Absences by Tenant

Tenant will notify Landlord in advance if Tenant will be away from the premises for _____ or more consecutive days. During such absence, Landlord may enter the premises at times reasonably necessary to maintain the property and inspect for needed repairs.

Several states with statutes that otherwise protect a tenant's privacy by requiring notice before entry (except in case of emergency) give landlords the specific legal right to enter the rental unit during a tenant's extended absence to maintain the property as necessary and to inspect for damage and needed repairs. Extended absence is often defined as seven days or more. For example, if you live in a cold-weather place and temperatures take a dive, it makes sense to check the pipes in rental units (to make sure they haven't burst) when the tenant is away for winter vacation.

While many states do not address this issue, you should be on safe legal ground to enter rental property during a tenant's extended absence, as long as you have a genuine reason to enter to protect the property from damage. You should enter only if something really needs to be done—that is, something the tenant would do if he were home, as part of his obligation to keep the property clean, safe and in good repair.

To protect yourself, include Clause 16, which requires that the tenant notify you when leaving your property for an extended time and alerts the tenant of your intent to enter the premises during these times if necessary.

How to Fill In Clause 16:

In the blank, fill in the time frame that you think is reasonable to provide the tenant advance notice of entry. Ten or fourteen days is common.

Clause 17. Possession of the Premises

a. *Tenant's failure to take possession.*
   If, after signing this Agreement, Tenant fails to take possession of the premises, Tenant will still be responsible for paying rent and complying with all other terms of this Agreement.

b. *Landlord's failure to deliver possession.*
   If Landlord is unable to deliver possession of the premises to Tenant for any reason not within Landlord's control, including, but not limited to, partial or complete destruction of the premises, Tenant will have the right to terminate this Agreement upon proper notice as required by law. In such event, Landlord's liability to Tenant will be limited to the return of all sums previously paid by Tenant to Landlord.

The first part of this clause (part a) explains that a tenant who chooses not to move in after signing the lease or rental agreement will still be required to pay rent and satisfy other conditions of the agreement. This does not mean, however, that you can sit back and expect to collect rent for the entire lease or rental agreement term. (As we explain in Chapter 5, you generally must take reasonably prompt steps to re-rent the premises, and you must credit the rent you collect against the first tenant's rent obligation.)

The second part of the clause (part b) protects you if you're unable, for reasons beyond your control, to turn over possession after having signed the agreement or lease—for example, if a fire spreads from next door and destroys the premises. It limits your financial liability to the new tenant to the return of any prepaid rent and security deposits (the "sums previously paid" in the language of the clause).

⚠️ **Clause 17 may not limit your liability if you cannot deliver possession because the old tenant is still on the premises—even if he is the subject of an eviction that you ultimately win.** *When a holdover tenant prevents the new tenant from moving in, landlords are often sued by the new tenant for not only the return of any prepaid rent and security deposits, but also the costs of temporary housing, storage costs and other losses. In some states, an attempt in the lease to limit the new tenant's recovery to the return of prepaid sums alone would not hold up in court. To protect yourself, you will want to shift some of the financial liability to the holdover tenant. You'll have a stronger chance of doing this if the old tenant has given written notice of his intent to move out. (See Clause 4, above, which requires written notice.)*

How to Fill In Clause 17:

You do not need to add anything to this clause.

Clause 18. Tenant Rules and Regulations

☐ Tenant acknowledges receipt of, and has read a copy of, tenant rules and regulations, which are attached to and incorporated into this Agreement by this reference.

Many landlords don't worry about detailed rules and regulations, especially when they rent single-family homes or duplexes. However, in larger buildings with many tenants, rules are usually important to control the use of common areas and equipment—both for the convenience, safety and welfare of the tenants and as a way to protect your property from damage. Rules and regulations also help avoid confusion and misunderstandings about day-to-day issues such as garbage disposal.

Not every minor rule needs to be incorporated in your lease or rental agreement. But it is a good idea to specifically incorporate important ones (especially those that are likely to be ignored by some tenants). Doing so gives you the authority to evict a tenant who persists in seriously violating your code of tenant rules and regulations. Also, to avoid charges of illegal discrimination, rules and regulations should apply equally to all tenants in your rental property.

Because tenant rules and regulations are often lengthy and may be revised occasionally, we suggest you prepare a separate attachment. (See sidebar, "How to Prepare Attachment Pages," at the beginning of this section.) Be sure the rules and regulations (including any revisions) are dated on each page and signed by both you and the tenant.

What's Covered in Tenant Rules and Regulations

Tenant rules and regulations typically cover issues such as:

- elevator safety and use
- pool rules
- garbage disposal and recycling
- vehicles and parking regulations—for example, restrictions of repairs on the premises or types of vehicles (such as no RVs)
- lock-out and lost key charges
- pet rules
- no smoking in common areas
- security system use
- specific details on what's considered excessive noise
- dangerous materials—nothing explosive should be on the premises
- storage of bikes, baby strollers and other equipment in halls, stairways and other common areas
- specific landlord and tenant maintenance responsibilities (such as stopped-up toilets or garbage disposals, broken windows, rodent and pest control, lawn and yard maintenance)
- use of the grounds and recreation areas
- maintenance of balconies and decks (for instance, no drying clothes on balconies)
- display of signs in windows
- laundry room rules
- waterbeds.

How to Fill In Clause 18:

If you have a set of Tenant Rules and Regulations, check the box. If you do not, simply put a line through this clause or write the words "N/A" or "Not Applicable."

Clause 19. Payment of Court Costs and Attorney Fees in a Lawsuit

In any action or legal proceeding to enforce any part of this Agreement, the prevailing party ☐ shall not/ ☐ shall recover reasonable attorney fees and court costs.

Many landlords assume that if they sue a tenant and win, the court will order the losing tenant to pay the landlord's court costs (filing fees, service of process charges, deposition costs and so on) and attorney fees. This is not generally true. In most states, a court will order the losing tenant to pay your attorney fees only if a written agreement specifically provides for it.

If, however, you have an "attorney fees" clause in your lease, all this changes. If you hire a lawyer to bring a lawsuit and win, the judge will order your tenant to pay your costs and attorney fees. (In rare instances, a court will order the loser to pay costs and fees on its own if it finds that the behavior of the losing party was particularly egregious.)

But there's another important issue you need to know about: By law in many states, an attorney fees clause in a lease or a rental agreement works both ways, even if you haven't written it that way. That is, even if the lease states only that you are entitled to attorney fees if you win a lawsuit, your tenants will be entitled to collect their attorney fees from you if they prevail. The amount you would be ordered to pay would be whatever the judge decides is reasonable.

So, especially if you live in a state that will read a "one-way" attorney fees clause as a two-way street, give some thought to whether you want to bind both of you to paying for the winner's costs and fees. Remember, if you can't actually collect a judgment containing attorney fees from an evicted tenant (which often happens), the clause will not help you. But if the tenant prevails, you will be stuck paying his costs and fees. In addition, the presence of a two-way clause will make it far easier for a tenant to secure a willing lawyer for even a doubtful claim, because the source of the lawyer's fee (you, if you lose) will probably appear more financially solid than if the client were paying the bill himself.

Especially if you intend to do all or most of your own legal work in any potential eviction or other lawsuit, you will almost surely be better off not to allow for attorney fees. Why? Because if the tenant wins, you will have to pay her fees; but if you win, she will owe you nothing, since you didn't hire an attorney. You can't even recover for the long hours you spent preparing for and handling the case.

Finally, be aware that attorney fees clauses only cover lawsuits concerning the meaning or implementation of the lease—such as a dispute about rent, security deposits or your right to access. An attorney fees clause would not apply in a personal injury or discrimination lawsuit.

How to Fill In Clause 19:

If you don't want to allow for attorney fees, check the box before the words "shall not" and cross out the word "shall."

If you want to be entitled to attorney fees and costs if you win—and you're willing to pay them if you lose—check the box before the word "shall" and cross out the words "shall not."

Clause 20.   Disclosures

Tenant acknowledges that Landlord has made the following disclosures regarding the premises:

☐ Disclosure of Information on Lead-Based Paint and/or Lead-Based Paint Hazards

☐ Other disclosures:

_____

_____

_____

Federal, state or local laws may require you to make certain disclosures before a new tenant signs a lease or rental agreement or moves in.

Lead Disclosures

If your rental unit was built prior to 1978, before signing a lease or rental agreement, you must tell new tenants about any known lead-based paint or lead-based paint hazards in the rental premises. You must also give them an EPA pamphlet, *Protect Your Family From Lead in Your Home*. This is a requirement of the Residential Lead-Based Paint Hazard Reduction Act, commonly known as Title X (42 U.S.C. § 4852d), which is administered by the U.S. Environmental Protection Agency (EPA).

In addition, both you and the tenant must sign an EPA-approved form—Disclosure of Information on Lead-Based Paint and/or Lead-Based Paint Hazards—that will prove that you told your tenants what you know about these hazards on your premises. You must keep the disclosure form as part of your records for three years from the date of the start of the tenancy.

As discussed below, state laws on lead disclosure may also come into play

Appendix 2 includes a blank tear-out copy of the Disclosure of Information on Lead-Based Paint and/or Lead-Based Paint Hazards form, and the EPA pamphlet Protect Your Family From Lead in Your Home *(both in English and in Spanish).*

⚠ Penalties are severe.
Property owners who fail to comply with EPA regulations for disclosing lead-based paint hazards face penalties of up to $10,000 for each violation and treble (triple) damages if a tenant is injured by your willful noncompliance.

Rental Properties Exempt From Title X Regulations

- housing built after January 1978
- housing certified lead-free by an accredited lead inspector
- lofts, efficiencies and studios
- short-term vacation rentals
- a single room rented in a residential dwelling
- housing designed for persons with disabilities, unless children under age six are present
- retirement communities (housing designed for seniors, where one or more tenant is at least 62 years old), unless children under age six are present.

Resources: Lead

Copies of Title X regulations and background information may be obtained by calling the National Lead Information Center at 800-424-LEAD, or checking its website, www.epa.gov/lead/nlic.htm. Information on the evaluation and control of lead may be obtained from the regional offices of the EPA, or the EPA website, www.epa.gov.

Some states require property owners to disclose lead hazards to prospective tenants. If a state statute is more protective of the tenant than the federal standard under Title X, you must follow the state statute. Alternatively, your state may choose to develop its own form, as long as it is consistent with the EPA model. Check with your state housing department or local office of the U.S. Department of Housing and Urban Development (HUD) to find out if this applies to you.

Disclosures of Hidden Defects

If there is any hidden (not obvious) aspect of your property that could cause injury or substantially interfere with a tenant's safe enjoyment and use of the dwelling—for example, an elevator that may be dangerous—your best bet is to fix it. If this is impossible, you are likely to be better off legally (should a future problem develop) if you disclose the defective or dangerous condition before the tenant signs the lease or rental agreement.

Landlords have a duty to warn tenants and others about naturally occurring dangers (such as loose soil) and man-made dangers (like low doorways or steep stairs) that are hidden but which you know (or should know) about. Disclose hidden defects in Clause 20 of your lease or rental agreement, so that it can never be claimed that a tenant was not warned of a potentially dangerous condition. For example, if the building contains asbestos insulation that could be dangerous if anyone made a hole in the wall, disclose this to your tenants. If appropriate, also post warning signs near hazards, such as a ramp that's slippery when wet or a tree that drops entire strips of bark during windy weather.

While disclosure doesn't guarantee that you won't be legally liable (also make sure your insurance protects you), it will likely help. Putting the tenant on notice that a problem exists will help prevent injuries and limit your liability should an injury occur from a defective condition in the rental unit or on the premises.

> ⚠️ **Some problems need to be fixed, not merely disclosed.**
> *Warning your tenants about a hidden defect does not absolve you of legal responsibility if the condition makes the dwelling uninhabitable or unreasonably dangerous. For example, you are courting liability if you rent an apartment with a gas heater that you know might blow up, even if you warn the tenant that the heater is faulty. Nor can you simply warn your tenants about prior crime on the premises and then fail to do anything (like installing deadbolts or hiring security) to promote safety.*

Other Disclosures

State laws may impose disclosure requirements, too, such as the need to inform tenants of the name and address of the bank where their security deposit is held. (Clause 8 covers security deposits.) Local rent control ordinances often require disclosures such as the name and address of the government agency or elected board that administers the ordinance. Here is a sampling of other state disclosure laws. This is not an exhaustive list. Check your state and local laws for details on these and other disclosure requirements:

- property located near former military ordnance (Cal. Civ. Code § 1940.7)
- tenant's gas or electric meter serves areas outside of the rental unit (Cal. Civ. Code § 1940.9 and Ill. Comp. Stat. §§ 735/1.2 and 740/5)
- full explanation of utility rates, charges and services (Iowa Code Ann. § 562A.13(4))
- existence of a state Department of Justice database that the tenant can access to learn if an individual is a registered sexual offender living within a community and zip code (Cal. Civ. Code § 2079.10a)
- fire safety and protection information (Fla. Statutes Annotated § 83.50 and Wash. Rev. Code Ann. § 59.18.060).
- rental unit has been flooded within the past five years (Ga. Code Ann. § 44-7-20 and (Okla. Stat. Ann. tit. 41, § 113a)
- landlord's excise tax number, so that tenants may file for a low-income tax credit (Haw. Rev. Stat. § 521-43)
- outstanding inspection orders, condemnation orders or declarations that the property is unfit. Citations for violations that do not involve threats to tenant health or safety must be summarized and posted in an obvious place, and the original must be available for review by the tenant. (Minn. Stat. Ann. § 504B.195)
- presence of dangerous mold (Cal. Health & Safety Code § 26147) or of any "controlled substances" releases, such as waste from illegal drug labs, on or under the residential property (Cal. Civ. Code § 1940.7.5).

How to Fill In Clause 20:

If your rental property was built before 1978, you must meet federal lead disclosure requirements, so check the first box and follow the advice above.

If you are legally required to make other disclosures as described above, check the second box and provide details in the blank space, adding additional pages as necessary. (See sidebar, "How to Prepare Attachment Pages," at the beginning of this section.)

Clause 21. Authority to Receive Legal Papers

The Landlord, any person managing the premises and anyone designated by the Landlord are authorized to accept service of process and receive other notices and demands, which may be delivered to:

☐ The Landlord, at the following address:_____

_____

☐ The manager, at the following address:_____

_____

☐ The following person, at the following address:_____

_____

It's the law in many states, and a good idea in all, to give your tenants information about everyone whom you have authorized to receive notices and legal papers, such as a tenant's notice that she is ending the tenancy or a tenant's court documents as part of an eviction defense. Of course, you may want to handle all of this yourself or delegate it to a manager or management company. Make sure the person you designate to receive legal papers is almost always available to receive tenant notices and legal papers. Also, be sure to keep your tenants up to date on any changes in this information.

How to Fill In Clause 21:

Provide your name and street address or the name and address of someone else you authorize to receive notices and legal papers on your behalf, such as a property manager.

Clause 22. Additional Provisions

Additional provisions are as follows:_____

_____

In this clause, you may list any additional provisions or agreements that are unique to you and the particular tenant signing the lease or rental agreement, such as a provision that prohibits smoking in the tenant's apartment or in the common areas.

If you don't have a separate Rules and Regulations clause (see Clause 18, above), you may spell out a few rules under this clause—for example, regarding lost key charges or use of a pool on the property.

How to Fill In Clause 22:

List additional provisions or rules here or in an attachment. (See sidebar, "How to Prepare Attachment Pages," at the beginning of this section.) If there are no additional provisions, write "N/A" or "Not Applicable."

There is no legal or practical imperative to put every small detail you want to communicate to the tenant into your lease or rental agreement.
Instead, prepare a welcoming, but no-nonsense, "move-in letter" that dovetails with the lease or rental agreement and highlights important terms of the tenancy—for example, how and where to report maintenance problems. You may also use a move-in letter to cover issues not included in the lease or rental agreement—for example, rules for use of a laundry room. (Chapter 4 covers move-in letters.)

Do not include exculpatory ("If there's a problem, I'm not responsible") clauses or hold harmless ("If there's a problem, you are responsible") clauses.
Many form leases include provisions that attempt to absolve you in advance from responsibility for your legal misdeeds. For example, one lease form generated by a popular software package contains a broad provision stating that you are not responsible for injuries to tenants and guests, even those you cause intentionally. Many exculpatory clauses are blatantly illegal: If a tenant is injured because of a dangerous condition you failed to fix for several months, no boilerplate lease provision will protect you from civil—and probably criminal—charges.

Clause 23. Validity of Each Part

If any portion of this Agreement is held to be invalid, its invalidity will not affect the validity or enforceability of any other provision of this Agreement.

This clause is known as a "savings" clause, and it is commonly used in contracts. It means that, in the unlikely event that one of the other clauses in the Agreement is found to be invalid by a court, the remainder of the Agreement will remain in force.

How to Fill In Clause 23:

You do not need to add anything to this clause.

Clause 24. Grounds for Termination of Tenancy

The failure of Tenant or Tenant's guests or invitees to comply with any term of this Agreement is grounds for termination of the tenancy, with appropriate notice to Tenant and procedures as required by law.

This clause states that any violation of the Agreement by the tenant, or by the tenant's business or social guests, is grounds for terminating the tenancy, according to the procedures established by your state or local laws. Making the tenant responsible for the actions of his guests can be extremely important—for example, if you discover that the tenant's family or friends are using or dealing illegal drugs on the premises or have damaged the property.

How to Fill In Clause 24:

You do not need to add anything to this clause.

Clause 25. Entire Agreement

This document constitutes the entire Agreement between the parties, and no promises or representations, other than those contained here and those implied by law, have been made by Landlord or Tenant. Any modifications to this Agreement must be in writing signed by Landlord and Tenant.

This clause establishes that the lease or rental agreement and any attachments (such as Rules and Regulations) constitute the entire agreement between you and your tenant. It means that oral promises (by you or the tenant) to do something different with respect to any aspect of the rental are not binding. Any changes or additions must be in writing. (Chapter 5, Section A discusses how to modify signed rental agreements and leases.)

How to Fill In Clause 25:

You do not need to add anything to this clause.

C. Signing the Lease or Rental Agreement

Make a copy of the lease or rental agreement, including all attachments. You and each tenant should sign both copies. At the end of the lease or rental agreement, there's space to include your signature, street address and phone number, or that of the person you authorize as your agent, such as a property manager. There's also space for the tenants' signatures and phone numbers.

Again, as stressed in Clause 1, make sure all adults living in the rental unit, including both members of a married couple, sign the lease or rental agreement. And check that the tenant's name and signature match his or her driver's license or other legal document.

If the tenant has a cosigner (see sidebar, "About Cosigners," below), you'll need to add a line for the cosigner's signature.

If you alter our form by writing or typing in changes, be sure that you and all tenants initial the changes when you sign the document, so as to forestall any possibility that a tenant will claim you unilaterally inserted changes after he or she signed.

⚠️ **Don't sign a lease until all terms are final and the tenant understands what's expected.**
All of your expectations should be written into the lease or rental agreement (or any attachments, such as Rules and Regulations) before you and the tenant sign the document. Never sign an incomplete document assuming last-minute changes can be made later. And be sure your tenant clearly understands the lease or rental agreement before signing (this may mean you'll need to review it clause by clause). Chapter 4 discusses how to get your new tenancy off to the right start.

Give one copy of the signed lease or rental agreement to the tenant(s), and keep the other one for your files. (If you are renting to more than one tenant, you don't need to prepare a separate agreement for each cotenant. After the agreement is signed, cotenants may make their own copies of the signed document.)

💡 Help tenants understand the lease or rental agreement before they sign it.
Too many landlords thrust a lease or rental agreement at tenants and expect them to sign it unread. Far better to encourage tenants to ask questions about anything that's unclear, or to actually review each clause with new tenants. It will save you lots of hassles later on.

If English is not a tenant's first language—especially if you regularly rent to people in the tenant's ethnic group—prepare and give the tenant a written translation. Appendix 2 includes a Spanish version of our lease and rental agreement. Some states require this. California, for example, requires landlords to notify Spanish-speaking tenants, in Spanish, of the right to request a Spanish version. But even if it's not legally required, you want your tenants to know and follow the rules. Providing a written translation of your lease or rental agreement is a great way to establish rapport with tenants.

About Cosigners

Some landlords require cosigners on rental agreements and leases, especially when renting to students who depend on parents for much of their income. The cosigner signs a separate agreement or the rental agreement or lease, under which she agrees to cover any rent or damage-repair costs the tenant fails to pay.

In practice, a cosigner's promise to guarantee the tenant's rent obligation may have less legal value than at first you might think. This is because the threat of eviction is the primary factor that motivates a tenant to pay the rent, and, obviously, you cannot evict a cosigner. Also, since the cosigner must be sued separately in either a regular civil lawsuit or in small claims court, actually doing so—for example, if a tenant stiffs you for a month's rent—may be more trouble than it's worth. This is especially true if the cosigner lives in another state, since the amount of money you are out will rarely justify hiring a lawyer and collecting a judgment.

In sum, the benefits of having a lease or rental agreement cosigned by someone who won't be living on the property are largely psychological. But these benefits may still be worth something: A tenant who thinks you can (and will) notify and

sue a cosigning relative or friend may be less likely to default on the rent. Similarly, a cosigner asked to pay the tenant's debts may persuade the tenant to pay.

If you decide to accept a cosigner, you may want to have that person fill out a separate rental application and agree to a credit check—after all, a cosigner who has no resources or connection to the tenant will be completely useless. Should the tenant and her prospective cosigner object to these inquiries and the costs of a credit check, you may wonder how serious they are about the guarantor's willingness to stand behind the tenant. Once you are satisfied that the cosigner can genuinely back up the tenant, add a line at the end of the lease or rental agreement for the dated signature, phone and address of the cosigner.

⚠ If you change the lease, have the cosigner sign the new version.
Generally speaking, a cosigner is bound only to the terms of the exact lease or rental agreement he cosigns. If you later change a significant term, add a new tenant or otherwise create a new contract, the original cosigner will probably be off the hook, unless you again get him to sign.

Month-to-Month Residential Rental Agreement

Clause 1.   Identification of Landlord and Tenant

This Agreement is entered into between _____ Marty Nelson _____

_____ ("Tenant") and

_____ Alex Stevens _____ ("Landlord").

Each Tenant is jointly and severally liable for the payment of rent and performance of all other terms of this Agreement.

Clause 2.   Identification of Premises

Subject to the terms and conditions in this Agreement, Landlord rents to Tenant, and Tenant rents from Landlord, for residential purposes only, the premises located at _____ 137 Howell St., Houston, Texas

_____ ("the premises"),

together with the following furnishings and appliances: _____

_____ .

Rental of the premises also includes _____

_____ .

Clause 3.   Limits on Use and Occupancy

The premises are to be used only as a private residence for Tenant(s) listed in Clause 1 of this Agreement, and their minor children. Occupancy by guests for more than _____ ten days every six months _____ is prohibited without Landlord's written consent and will be considered a breach of this Agreement.

Clause 4.   Term of the Tenancy

The rental will begin on _____ September 15 _____, 200 X _____, and continue on a month-to-month basis. Landlord may terminate the tenancy or modify the terms of this Agreement by giving the Tenant _____ 30 _____ days' written notice. Tenant may terminate the tenancy by giving the Landlord _____ 30 _____ days' written notice.

Clause 5.   Payment of Rent

Regular monthly rent.

Tenant will pay to Landlord a monthly rent of $_____ 900 _____, payable in advance on the first day of each month, except when that day falls on a weekend or legal holiday, in which case rent is due on the next business day. Rent will be paid in the following manner unless Landlord designates   . otherwise:

Delivery of payment.

Rent will be paid:

☒ by mail, to __Alex Stevens (address below)__

☐ in person, at _____

Form of payment.

Landlord will accept payment in these forms:

☒ personal check made payable to __Alex Stevens__

☒ cashier's check made payable to __Alex Stevens__

☐ credit card

☒ money order

☐ cash

Prorated first month's rent.

For the period from Tenant's move-in date, ____September 15____, 200_X_, through

the end of the month, Tenant will pay to Landlord the prorated monthly rent of $ _450_.

This amount will be paid on or before the date the Tenant moves in.

Clause 6.   Late Charges

If Tenant fails to pay the rent in full before the end of the ___third___ day after it's due, Tenant

will pay Landlord a late charge as follows: __$10, plus $5 for each additional day that the rent__

___remains unpaid. The total late charge for any one month will not exceed $45___.

Landlord does not waive the right to insist on payment of the rent in full on the date it is due.

Clause 7.   Returned Check and Other Bank Charges

If any check offered by Tenant to Landlord in payment of rent or any other amount due under this

Agreement is returned for lack of sufficient funds, a "stop payment" or any other reason, Tenant will pay

Landlord a returned check charge of $ _15_.

Clause 8.   Security Deposit

On signing this Agreement, Tenant will pay to Landlord the sum of $ _1,800_ as a security

deposit. Tenant may not, without Landlord's prior written consent, apply this security deposit to the last

month's rent or to any other sum due under this Agreement. Within ___30 days___

after Tenant has vacated the premises, returned keys and provided Landlord with a forwarding address,

Landlord will return the deposit in full or give Tenant an itemized written statement of the reasons for, and

the dollar amount of, any of the security deposit retained by Landlord, along with a check for any

deposit balance.

[optional clauses here, if any]

Clause 9.   Utilities

Tenant will pay all utility charges, except for the following, which will be paid by Landlord:

garbage and water _____

_____ .

Clause 10. Assignment and Subletting

Tenant will not sublet any part of the premises or assign this Agreement without the prior written consent of Landlord.

Clause 11. Tenant's Maintenance Responsibilities

Tenant will: (1) keep the premises clean, sanitary and in good condition and, upon termination of the tenancy, return the premises to Landlord in a condition identical to that which existed when Tenant took occupancy, except for ordinary wear and tear; (2) immediately notify Landlord of any defects or dangerous conditions in and about the premises of which Tenant becomes aware; and (3) reimburse Landlord, on demand by Landlord, for the cost of any repairs to the premises damaged by Tenant or Tenant's guests or business invitees through misuse or neglect.

Tenant has examined the premises, including appliances, fixtures, carpets, drapes and paint, and has found them to be in good, safe and clean condition and repair, except as noted in the Landlord/Tenant Checklist.

Clause 12. Repairs and Alterations by Tenant

a.   Except as provided by law, or as authorized by the prior written consent of Landlord, Tenant will not make any repairs or alterations to the premises, including nailing holes in the walls or painting the rental unit.

b.   Tenant will not, without Landlord's prior written consent, alter, re-key or install any locks to the premises or install or alter any burglar alarm system. Tenant will provide Landlord with a key or keys capable of unlocking all such re-keyed or new locks as well as instructions on how to disarm any altered or new burglar alarm system.

Clause 13. Violating Laws and Causing Disturbances

Tenant is entitled to quiet enjoyment of the premises. Tenant and guests or invitees will not use the premises or adjacent areas in such a way as to: (1) violate any law or ordinance, including laws prohibiting the use, possession or sale of illegal drugs; (2) commit waste (severe property damage); or (3) create a nuisance by annoying, disturbing, inconveniencing or interfering with the quiet enjoyment and peace and quiet of any other tenant or nearby resident.

Clause 14. Pets

No animal, bird or other pet will be kept on the premises, even temporarily, except properly trained dogs needed by blind, deaf or disabled persons and _____

under the following conditions: _____

_____

_____ .

Clause 15. Landlord's Right to Access

Landlord or Landlord's agents may enter the premises in the event of an emergency, to make repairs or improvements or to show the premises to prospective buyers or tenants. Landlord may also enter the premises to conduct an annual inspection to check for safety or maintenance problems. Except in cases of emergency, Tenant's abandonment of the premises, court order or where it is impractical to do so, Landlord shall give Tenant _____ 24 hours' _____ notice before entering.

Clause 16. Extended Absences by Tenant

Tenant will notify Landlord in advance if Tenant will be away from the premises for __ seven ____ or more consecutive days. During such absence, Landlord may enter the premises at times reasonably necessary to maintain the property and inspect for needed repairs.

Clause 17. Possession of the Premises

a. Tenant's failure to take possession.

If, after signing this Agreement, Tenant fails to take possession of the premises, Tenant will still be responsible for paying rent and complying with all other terms of this Agreement.

b. Landlord's failure to deliver possession.

If Landlord is unable to deliver possession of the premises to Tenant for any reason not within Landlord's control, including, but not limited to, partial or complete destruction of the premises, Tenant will have the right to terminate this Agreement upon proper notice as required by law. In such event, Landlord's liability to Tenant will be limited to the return of all sums previously paid by Tenant to Landlord.

Clause 18. Tenant Rules and Regulations

☐   Tenant acknowledges receipt of, and has read a copy of, tenant rules and regulations, which are attached to and incorporated into this Agreement by this reference.

Clause 19. Payment of Court Costs and Attorney Fees in a Lawsuit

In any action or legal proceeding to enforce any part of this Agreement, the prevailing party
☐ shall not / ☒ shall recover reasonable attorney fees and court costs.

Clause 20. Disclosures

Tenant acknowledges that Landlord has made the following disclosures regarding the premises:

☐   Disclosure of Information on Lead-Based Paint and/or Lead-Based Paint Hazards

☐   Other disclosures:

_____

_____

_____

Clause 21. Authority to Receive Legal Papers

The Landlord, any person managing the premises and anyone designated by the Landlord are authorized to accept service of process and receive other notices and demands, which may be delivered to:

☒   The Landlord, at the following address: ___28 Franklin St., Houston, Texas 77002___

_____

☐   The manager, at the following address: _____

_____

☐   The following person, at the following address: _____

_____

Clause 22. Additional Provisions

Additional provisions are as follows: _____

_____

_____

_____

_____

_____

_____

_____ .

Clause 23. Validity of Each Part

If any portion of this Agreement is held to be invalid, its invalidity will not affect the validity or enforceability of any other provision of this Agreement.

Clause 24. Grounds for Termination of Tenancy

The failure of Tenant or guests or invitees to comply with any term of this Agreement is grounds for termination of the tenancy, with appropriate notice to Tenant and procedures as required by law.

Clause 25. Entire Agreement

This document constitutes the entire Agreement between the parties, and no promises or representations, other than those contained here and those implied by law, have been made by Landlord or Tenant. Any modifications to this Agreement must be in writing signed by Landlord and Tenant.

Sept. 1, 200X	*Alex Steven*	Landlord
Date	Landlord or Landlord's Agent	Title

28 Franklin St.	
Street Address	

Houston, Texas 77002	713-555-1578
City, State & Zip	Phone

Sept. 1, 200X	*Marty Nelson*	713-555-8751
Date	Tenant	Phone

_____	_____	_____
Date	Tenant	Phone

_____	_____	_____
Date	Tenant	Phone

Choosing Tenants: Your Most Important Decision

Choosing tenants is the most important decision any landlord makes. It should go almost without saying that to do it well and stay out of legal trouble, you need a good system. Follow the steps in this chapter to maximize your chances of selecting tenants who will pay their rent on time, keep their units in good condition and not cause you any legal or practical problems later.

Before you advertise your property for rent, make a number of basic decisions— including how much rent to charge, whether to offer a fixed-term lease or a month-to-month tenancy, how many tenants can occupy each rental unit, how big a security deposit to require and whether you'll allow pets. Making these important decisions should dovetail with writing your lease or rental agreement (see Chapter 2).

A. How to Advertise Rental Property

You can advertise rental property in many ways:
- putting an "Apartment for Rent" sign in front of the building or in one of the windows
- taking out classified newspaper ads
- posting flyers on neighborhood bulletin boards
- listing with a local homefinders' or apartment-finding service that provides a centralized listing of rental units for a particular geographic area
- listing with a local real estate broker that handles rentals
- buying ads in apartment rental guides or magazines
- hiring a property management company that will advertise your rentals as part of the management fee, or
- posting a notice online (see sidebar, "Online Apartment Listing Services," below, for details).

Online Apartment Listing Services

Dozens of online services now make it easy to reach potential tenants, whether they already live in your community or are mvoing from out of state.

Community posting boards allow you to list your rentals at no or low charge and are a good place to start. *Craigslist,* one of the most established community boards, has local sites for many major metropolitan areas, including San Francisco, New York City, Atlanta, Miami, Phoenix, Chicago, Washington, DC and Boston. Check out www.craigslist.org for details.

National apartment listing services are also available, with the largest ones representing millions of apartment units in the United States. Some of the most established are:
- www.homestore.com
- www.apartments.com
- www.rent.com
- www.apartmentguide.com, and
- www.forrent.com.

These national sites offer a wide range of services, from simple text-only ads that provide basic information on your rental (such as the number of bedrooms) to full-scale virtual tours and floor plans of the rental property. Prices vary widely depending on the type of ad, how long you want it to run and any services you purchase (some websites provide tenant-screening services).

What will work best depends on a number of factors, including the characteristics of the particular rental property (such as rent, size, amenities), its location, your budget and whether you are in a hurry to rent. Many smaller landlords find that instead of advertising widely and having to screen many potential tenants in an effort to sort the good from the bad, it makes better sense to market their rentals through word of mouth—telling friends, colleagues, neighbors and current tenants. After all, people who already live in your property will want decent neighbors.

But no matter how you let people know about the availability of your rental units, you want to follow these simple rules and stay out of legal hot water:

Describe the rental unit accurately. Your ad should be easy to understand and scrupulously honest. Also, as a practical matter, you should avoid abbreviations and real estate jargon in your ad. Include basic details, such as:

- rent
- size—particularly number of bedrooms and baths
- location—either the general neighborhood or street address
- lease or month-to-month rental agreement
- special features—such as fenced-in yard, view, washer/dryer, fireplace, remodeled kitchen, furnished, garage parking, doorman, hardwood floors or wall-to-wall carpeting
- phone number or email for more details (unless you're going to show the unit only at an open house and don't want to take calls), and
- date and time of any open house.

If you have any important rules (legal and nondiscriminatory, of course), such as no pets, put them in your ad. Letting prospective tenants know about your important policies can save you from talking to a lot of unsuitable people.

Be sure your ad can't be construed as discriminatory. The best way to do this is to focus only on the rental property—not on any particular type of tenant. Specifically, ads should never mention sex, race, religion, disability or age (unless yours is legally sanctioned senior citizens housing). And ads should never imply through words, photographs or illustrations that you prefer to rent to people because of their age, sex or race. (Section E, below, covers antidiscrimination laws.)

Quote an honest price in your ad. Or, put another way, if a tenant who is otherwise acceptable (has a good credit history and impeccable references and meets all the criteria laid out in Section D, below), shows up promptly and agrees to all the terms set out in your ad, he or she should be able to rent your property for the price you have advertised. By contrast, if you suddenly find a reason why it will cost significantly more, you are likely to be in violation of your state's false advertising laws. This doesn't mean you are always legally required to rent at your advertised price, however. If a tenant asks for more services or significantly different lease terms that you feel require more rent, it's fine to bargain and raise your price, as long as your proposed increase doesn't violate any local rent control laws.

Don't advertise something you don't have. Some large landlords, management companies and rental services have advertised units that weren't really available in order to produce a large number of prospective tenants who could then be directed to higher-priced or inferior units. Such bait-and-switch advertising is clearly illegal under consumer fraud laws, and many property owners have been prosecuted for such practices.

Don't overhype security measures. Don't exaggerate your written or oral description of security measures. Not only will you have begun the landlord-tenant relationship on a note of insincerity, but your descriptions of security may legally obligate you to actually provide what you have portrayed. Or, if you fail to do so, or fail to conscientiously maintain promised security measures in working order (such as outdoor lighting or an electronic gate on the parking garage), a court or jury may find your failure to be a material factor allowing a crime to occur on the premises. And, if this happens, chances are good you will be held liable for a tenant's losses or injuries.

B. Renting Property That's Still Occupied

Often, you can wait until the old tenant moves out to show a rental unit to prospective tenants. This gives you the chance to refurbish the unit and avoids problems such as promising the place to a new tenant, only to have the existing tenant not move out on time or leave the place a mess.

To eliminate any gap in rent, however, you may want to show a rental unit while its current tenants are still there. This can create a conflict; in most states, you have a right to show the still-occupied property to prospective tenants, but your current tenants are still entitled to a reasonable level of privacy. (For details, see Clause 15 of the lease and rental agreement in Chapter 2.)

To minimize disturbing your current tenant, follow these guidelines:

- Before implementing your plans to find a new tenant, discuss them with outgoing tenants so you can be as accommodating as possible.
- Give current tenants as much notice as possible before entering and showing a rental unit to prospective tenants.
- Try to limit the number of times you show the unit in a given week, and make sure your current tenants agree to any evening and weekend visits.
- Consider reducing the rent slightly for the existing tenant if showing the unit really will be an imposition.
- If possible, avoid putting a sign on the rental property itself, since this almost guarantees that your existing tenants will be bothered by strangers. Or, if you can't avoid putting up a sign, make sure any sign clearly warns against disturbing the occupant and includes a telephone number for information. Something on the order of "For Rent: Shown by Appointment Only. Call 555-1700. Do Not Disturb Occupants" should work fine.

If, despite your best efforts to protect their privacy, the current tenants are uncooperative or hostile, it really is best to avoid legal hassles and wait until they leave before showing the unit. Also, if the current tenant is a complete slob or has damaged the place, you'll be far better off to apply paint and elbow grease before trying to re-rent it.

C. Dealing With Prospective Tenants

It's good business, as well as a sound way to protect yourself from future legal problems, to carefully screen prospective tenants. To avoid legal problems and choose the best tenant, ask all prospective tenants to fill out a written rental application that includes information on the applicant's employment, income, credit and rental housing history, including up-to-date references. It's legal and a good idea to ask for the applicant's Social Security and driver's license numbers. You can also ask if the applicant has declared bankruptcy, been evicted or been convicted of a crime. (You'll also get much of this information from a credit report, as discussed in Section D3, below.)

A sample Rental Application is shown below, and a blank tear-out version is in Appendix 2 at the back of this book.

Before giving prospective tenants a Rental Application, complete the box at the top, filling in the property address, the rental term and any deposit or credit check fee that tenants must pay before moving in. (Section D3, below, discusses credit check fees.)

Here are some basic guidelines for accepting rental applications:

- Each prospective tenant—everyone age 18 or older who wants to live in your rental property —should completely fill out a separate written application. This is true whether you're renting to a married couple or to unrelated roommates, a complete stranger or the cousin of your current tenant.

- Always make sure that prospective tenants complete the entire Rental Application, including Social Security number, driver's license or other identifying information (such as a passport number), current employment, bank and emergency contacts. You may need this information later to track down a tenant who skips town leaving unpaid rent or abandoned property. Also, you may need the So-cial Security number or other identifying information, such as a passport, to request an applicant's credit report.

- Request proof of identity and immigration status. In these security-sensitive times, many landlords ask prospective tenants to show their driver's license or other photo identification as a way to verify that the applicant is using his real name. You may also ask applicants for proof of identity and eligibility to work under U.S. immigration laws, such as a passport or naturalization certificate, using Form I-9 (Employment Eligibility Verification) of the Bureau of Citizenship and Immigration Services or BCIS (formerly Immigration and Naturalization Service or INS). This form (and instructions for completing it) are available from the BCIS website at www.immigration.gov, or by phone at 800-375-5283. Under federal fair housing laws, you may not selectively ask for such immigration information—that is, you must ask all prospective tenants, not just those you suspect may be in the country illegally. It is illegal to discriminate on the basis of national origin.

- Be sure all potential tenants sign the Rental Application, authorizing you to verify the information and references. (Some employers and banks require written authorization before they will talk to you.) You may also want to prepare a separate authorization, so that you don't need to copy the entire application and send it off every time a bank or employer wants proof that the tenant authorized you to verify the information.

A sample Consent to Background and Reference Check is shown below, and Appendix 2 includes a blank tear-out copy.

Rental Application

SEPARATE APPLICATION REQUIRED FROM EACH APPLICANT AGE 18 OR OLDER.

THIS SECTION TO BE COMPLETED BY LANDLORD

Address of Property to Be Rented: _178 West 81st St., Apt. 4F_

Rental Term: ☐ month-to-month ☒ lease from _March 1, 200X_ to _February 28, 200X_

Amounts Due Prior to Occupancy

First month's rent .... $ _1,500_

Security deposit .... $ _1,500_

Credit check fee .... $ _30_

Other (specify): _Broker's fee_ $ _1,500_

TOTAL .... $ _4,530_

APPLICANT

Full Name—include all names you use(d): _Hannah Silver_

Home Phone: (_609_) _555-3789_ Work Phone: (_609_) _555-4567_

Social Security Number: _123-000-4567_ Driver's License Number/State: _NJD123456_

Other Identifying Information: _____

Vehicle Make: _Toyota_ Model: _Tercel_ Color: _White_ Year: _1994_

License Plate Number/State: _NJ1234567_

ADDITIONAL OCCUPANTS

List everyone, including children, who will live with you:

Full Name	Relationship to Applicant
Dennis Olson	Husband

RENTAL HISTORY

Current Address: 39 Maple St., Princeton, NJ 08540

Dates Lived at Address: May 1996–date   Reason for Leaving: New job in NYC

Landlord/Manager: Jane Tucker   Landlord/Manager's Phone: (609) 555-7523

Previous Address: 1215 Middlebrook Lane, Princeton, NJ 08540

Dates Lived at Address: June 1987-May 1996   Reason for Leaving: Better apartment

Landlord/Manager: Ed Palermo   Landlord/Manager's Phone: (609) 555-3711

Previous Address: 1527 Highland Dr., New Brunswick, NJ 08444

Dates Lived at Address: Jan. 1986–June 1987   Reason for Leaving: Wanted to live closer to work

EMPLOYMENT HISTORY

Name and Address of Current Employer: Argonworks, 54 Nassau St., Princeton, NJ

Phone: (609) 555-2333

Name of Supervisor: Tom Schmidt   Supervisor's Phone: (609) 555-2333

Dates Employed at This Job: 1993–date   Position or Title: Marketing Director

Name and Address of Previous Employer: Princeton Times
13 Junction Rd., Princeton, NJ   Phone: (609) 555-1111

Name of Supervisor: Dory Krossber   Supervisor's Phone: (609) 555-2366

Dates Employed at This Job: June 1992–Feb. 1993   Position or Title: Marketing Assistant

INCOME

1. Your gross monthly employment income (before deductions): $ 6,000

2. Average monthly amounts of other income (specify sources): $ _____

   Note: This does not include my husband's income.

   See his application.

                    TOTAL: $ 6,000

CREDIT AND FINANCIAL INFORMATION

Bank/Financial Accounts	Account Number	Bank/Institution	Branch
Savings Account:	1222345	N.J. Federal	Trenton, NJ
Checking Account:	789101	Princeton S&L	Princeton, NJ
Money Market or Similar Account:	234789	City Bank	Princeton, NJ

Credit Accounts & Loans	Type of Account (Auto loan, Visa, etc.)	Account Number	Name of Creditor	Amount Owed	Monthly Payment
Major Credit Card:	Visa	123456	City Bank	$1,000	$500
Major Credit Card:	Dept. Store	45789	Macy	$500	$500
Loan (mortgage, car,					
student loan, etc.):					
Other Major Obligations:					

MISCELLANEOUS

Describe the number and type of pets you want to have in the rental property:

None now, but we might want to get a cat some time

Describe water-filled furniture you want to have in the rental property:

Do you smoke? ☐ yes ☒ no

Have you ever: Filed for bankruptcy? ☐ yes ☒ no   Been sued? ☐ yes ☒ no

Been evicted? ☐ yes ☒ no   Been convicted of a crime? ☐ yes ☒ no

Explain any "yes" listed above:

REFERENCES AND EMERGENCY CONTACT

Personal Reference: __Joan Stanley__   Relationship: __Friend, coworker__

Address: __785 Spruce St., Princeton, NJ 08540__

_____ Phone: __(609) 555-4578__

Personal Reference: __Marnie Swatt__   Relationship: __Friend__

Address: __82 East 59th St., #12B, NYC__

_____ Phone: __(212) 555-8765__

Contact in Emergency: __Connie & Martin Silver__   Relationship: __Parents__

Address: __7852 Pierce St., Somerset, NJ 08321__

_____ Phone: __(609) 555-7878__

I certify that all the information given above is true and correct and understand that my lease or rental

agreement may be terminated if I have made any material false or incomplete statements in this application.

I authorize verification of the information provided in this application from my credit sources, credit bureaus,

current and previous landlords and employers and personal references.

__February 15, 200X__   _Hannah Silver_

Date   Applicant

Notes (Landlord/Manager): _____

_____

_____

_____

_____

_____

_____

_____

_____

_____

_____

Consent to Background and Reference Check

I authorize _____ Jan Gold _____ to obtain information about me

from my credit sources, credit bureaus, current and previous landlords and employers and personal

references. I authorize my credit sources, credit bureaus, current and previous landlords and employers

and personal references to disclose to _____ Jan Gold _____

such information about me that is relevant to _____ Jan Gold _____'s evaluation of me as a

prospective tenant.

_____ Michael Clark _____
Name

_____ 123 State Street, Chicago, Illinois _____
Address

_____ 312-555-9876 _____
Phone Number

_____ February 2, 200X _____   _Michael Clark_ _____
Date   Applicant

D. Checking References, Credit History and More

If an application looks good, your next step is to follow up thoroughly. The time and money you spend are some of the most cost-effective expenditures you'll ever make.

⚠ Be consistent in your screening.
You risk a charge of illegal discrimination if you screen certain categories of applicants more stringently than others—for example, only requiring credit reports from racial minorities. Section E, below, discusses how to avoid illegal discrimination.

Here are six steps of a very thorough screening process. You should always go through at least the first three to check out the applicant's previous landlords and income and employment and run a credit check.

1. Check With Previous Landlords and Other References

Always call previous landlords or managers for references—even if you have a written letter of reference from a previous landlord. It's worth the cost of a long-distance phone call to weed out a tenant who may cause problems down the road. Also call employers and personal references listed on the application.

To organize the information you gather from these calls, use the Tenant References form, which lists key questions to ask previous landlords, employers and other references. Be sure to take notes of all your conversations and keep them on file. You may note your reasons for refusing an individual on this form—for example, negative credit information, bad references from a previous landlord or your inability to verify information. You'll want a record of this information so that you can survive a fair housing challenge if a rejected applicant files a discrimination complaint against you.

A sample Tenant References screening form is shown below, and Appendix 2 includes a blank tear-out copy of the form.

2. Verify Income and Employment

Obviously, you want to make sure that all tenants have the income to pay the rent each month. Call the prospective tenant's employer to verify income and length of employment. Make notes on the Tenant References form, discussed above.

Before providing this information, some employers require written authorization from the employee. You will need to mail or fax the employer a signed copy of the release included at the bottom of the Rental Application form or the separate Consent to Background and Reference Check form (see Section C, above). If for any reason you question the income information you get by telephone—for example, you suspect a buddy of the applicant is exaggerating on his behalf—you may also ask applicants for copies of recent paycheck stubs.

It's also reasonable to require documentation of other sources of income, such as Social Security, disability payments, workers' compensation, welfare, child support or alimony.

How much income is enough? Think twice before renting to someone if the rent will take more than one-third of their income, especially if they have a lot of debts.

3. Obtain a Credit Report

Private credit reporting agencies collect and sell credit files and other information about consumers. Many landlords find it essential to check a prospective tenant's credit history with at least one credit reporting agency to see how responsible the person is about managing money.

a. How to Get a Credit Report

A credit report contains a gold mine of information on a prospective tenant. You can find out, for example, if a particular person has a history of paying rent or bills late or has gone through bankruptcy, been convicted of a crime or ever been evicted. (Your legal right to get information on evictions, however, may vary from state to state.) Credit reports usually cover the past seven to ten years. To run a credit check, you'll normally need a prospective tenant's name, address and Social Security number.

If you own many rental properties and need credit reports frequently, consider joining one of the three largest credit reporting agencies—Equifax, Trans Union or Experian (formerly TRW)—which charge about $20 to $30 in annual fees plus $10 to $15 per report. You can find their numbers and those of other tenant-screening companies in the Yellow Pages under "Credit Reporting Agencies," or on the Internet under "Credit Report Services." Your state or local apartment association may also offer credit reporting services. With some credit reporting agencies, you can obtain an oral credit report the same day it's requested, and a written one within a day or two.

b. Credit Check Fees

It's legal in most states to charge prospective tenants a fee for the cost of the credit report itself and your time and trouble. Any credit check fee should be reasonably related to the cost of the credit check— $20 to $30 is common. Check your state law for any limits. California, for example, sets a maximum screening fee of $30 per applicant and requires landlords to provide an itemized receipt when accepting a credit check fee (Cal. Civ. Code § 1950.6).

Some landlords don't charge credit check fees, preferring to absorb the cost as they would any other cost of business. For low-end units, charging an extra fee can be a barrier to getting tenants in the first place, and a tenant who pays a fee but is later rejected is likely to be annoyed and possibly

Tenant References

Name of Applicant: ___Michael Clark___

Address of Rental Unit: ___123 State Street, Chicago, Illinois___

PREVIOUS LANDLORD OR MANAGER

Contact (name, property owner or manager, address of rental unit): ___Kate Steiner, 345 Mercer St.,___
___Chicago, (312) 555-5432___

Date: ___February 4, 200X___

QUESTIONS

When did tenant rent from you (move-in and move-out dates)? ___December 1998 to date___

What was the monthly rent? ___$850___　　　Did tenant pay rent on time? ___A week late a few times___

Was tenant considerate of neighbors—that is, no loud parties and fair, careful use of common areas?
___Yes, considerate___

Did tenant have any pets? If so, were there any problems? ___Yes, he had a cat, contrary to rental___
___agreement___

Did tenant make any unreasonable demands or complaints? ___No___

Why did tenant leave? ___He wants to live someplace that allows pets.___

Did tenant give the proper amount of notice before leaving? ___Yes___

Did tenant leave the place in good condition? Did you need to use the security deposit to cover damage?
___No problems___

Any particular problems you'd like to mention? ___No___

Would you rent to this person again? ___Yes, but without pets___

Other Comments:

EMPLOYMENT VERIFICATION

Contact (name, company, position): _Brett Field, Manager, Chicago Car Company_

Date: _February 5, 200X_ Salary: _$60,000_ Dates of Employment: _March 1996 to date_

Comments: _No problems. Fine employee. Michael is responsible and hard-working._

PERSONAL REFERENCE

Contact (name and relationship to applicant): _Sandy Cameron, friend_

Date: _February 5, 200X_ How long have you known the applicant? _Five years_

Would you recommend this person as a prospective tenant? _Yes_

Comments: _Michael is very neat and responsible. He's reliable and will be a great tenant._

CREDIT AND FINANCIAL INFORMATION

Mostly fine—see attached credit report.

NOTES (INCLUDING REASONS FOR REJECTING APPLICANT)

Applicant had a history of late rent payments and kept a cat, contrary to the rental agreement.

more apt to claim that you have rejected her for a discriminatory reason.

The Rental Application form in this book informs prospective tenants if you charge a credit check fee. Be sure prospective tenants understand that paying a credit check fee does not guarantee the tenant will get the rental unit.

💡 ***It's a mistake to collect a credit check fee from lots of people.***
If you expect a large number of applicants, you'd be wise not to accept fees from everyone. Instead, read over the applications first and do a credit check only on applicants you're seriously considering. That way, you won't waste your time (and prospective tenants' money) collecting fees from unqualified applicants.

⚠ ***It is generally illegal to charge a credit check fee if you do not use it for the stated purpose and pocket it instead.***
Return any credit check fees you don't use for that purpose.

c. What You're Looking For in a Credit Report

As you surely know, it makes sense to be leery of applicants with lots of debts—this clearly includes people whose monthly payments plus the rent obligation exceed 40% of their after-tax income. Also, look at the person's bill-paying habits, and, of course, pay attention to lawsuits and evictions.

Sometimes, your only choice is to rent to someone with poor or fair credit—or even no credit (for example, a student or recent graduate). If that's your situation, you should still adopt sensible screening requirements such as these:

- positive references from previous landlords and employers
- a creditworthy cosigner of the lease (see the discussion on cosigners at the end of Chapter 2)
- a good-sized deposit—as much as you can collect under state law and the market will

bear (see Clause 8 of the form agreements in Chapter 2), and
- proof of specific steps taken to improve bad credit—for example, enrollment in a debt counseling group.

4. Verify Bank Account Information

If an individual's credit history raises questions about financial stability, you may want to double-check the bank accounts listed on the rental application. If so, you'll probably need an authorization form such as the one included at the bottom of the Rental Application, or the separate Consent to Background and Reference Check form (discussed in Section C, above). Banks differ as to the type of information they will provide over the phone. Generally, without a written authorization, banks will only confirm that an individual has an account there and that it is in good standing.

⚠ ***Be wary of an applicant who has no checking or savings account.***
Tenants who offer to pay cash or with a money order should be viewed with extreme caution. Perhaps the individual bounced so many checks that the bank dropped the account or the income comes from a shady or illegitimate source—for example, from drug dealing.

5. Review Court Records

If your prospective tenant has previously lived in your area, you may want to review local court records to see if collection or eviction lawsuits have ever been filed against him. Checking court records may seem like overkill, since some of this information may be available on credit reports, but now and then it's an invaluable tool if you are able to weed out a prospective tenant who is almost sure to be a troublemaker. Especially if you fear that the person who rubs you the wrong way might accuse you of illegal discrimination if you turn down her application, you'll want to have good documentation of your decision. Because court records are kept for many years, this kind of information can supplement references from recent landlords. Talk to the court clerk at the local court that handles eviction cases for information on how to check court records.

6. Use Megan's Law to Check State Databases

Not surprisingly, most landlords do not want tenants with criminal records, particularly convictions for violent crimes or crimes against children. Checking a prospective tenant's credit report, as recommended above, is one way to find out about a person's criminal history. Self-reporting is another: Rental applications, such as the one in this book, typically ask whether the prospective tenant has ever been convicted of a crime. "Megan's Law" may also be a useful source of information. Named after a young girl who was killed by a convicted child molester who lived in her neighborhood, this federal crime prevention law charges the FBI with keeping a nationwide database of persons convicted of sexual offenses against minors and violent sexual offenses against anyone (42 U.S.C. §§ 14701 and following). Every state has its own version of Megan's Law that requires certain convicted sexual offenders to register with local law enforcement officials who keep a database on their whereabouts. For information on your access to this type of database, contact your local law enforcement agency.

E. Avoiding Illegal Discrimination

Federal and state antidiscrimination laws limit what you can say and do in the tenant selection process. Basically, you need to keep in mind three important points:

1. You are legally free to choose among pro-spective tenants as long as your decisions are based on legitimate business criteria. You are entitled to reject people for the following reasons:

- poor credit history
- income that you reasonably regard as insufficient to pay the rent
- negative references from previous landlords indicating problems—such as property damage or consistently late rent payments—that make someone a bad risk
- convictions for criminal offenses
- inability to meet the legal terms of a lease or rental agreement, such as someone who can't come up with the security deposit or who wants to keep a pet and your policy is no pets, or
- more people than you want to live in the unit—assuming that your limit on the number of tenants is clearly tied to health and safety or legitimate business needs. (See Clause 3 discussion of occupancy limits in Chapter 2.)

2. Antidiscrimination laws specify clearly illegal reasons to refuse to rent to a tenant. The federal Fair Housing Act (42 U.S.C. §§ 3601-3619) prohibits discrimination on the basis of race or color, religion, national origin, gender, age, familial status (children) and physical or mental disability (including recovering alcoholics and people with a past drug addiction). Many states and cities also prohibit discrimination based on marital status or sexual orientation.

For more information on the rules and regulations of the Fair Housing Act, contact HUD's Fair Housing Information Clearinghouse at 800-669-9777 or check the HUD website at www. hud.gov.

For information on state and local housing discrimination laws, contact your state fair housing agency. For a list of state agencies and contact information, see www.fairhousing.com/resources/finder/index.htm, a website maintained by the National Fair Housing Advocate Online.

3. Consistency is crucial when dealing with pro-spective tenants. If you don't treat all tenants more

The Rights of Disabled Tenants

The Fair Housing Act requires that landlords *accommodate* the needs of disabled tenants, at the landlord's own expense. (42 U.S.C. § 3604(f)(3)(B) (1988).) You are expected to adjust your rules, procedures or services in order to give a person with a disability an equal opportunity to use and enjoy a dwelling unit or a common space. Accommodations include such things as providing a close-in, spacious parking space for a wheelchair-bound tenant (assuming you provide parking). Your duty to accommodate disabled tenants does not mean that you must bend every rule and change every procedure at the tenant's request. You are expected to accommodate "reasonable" requests, but need not undertake changes that would seriously impair your ability to run your business.

The Fair Housing Act also requires landlords to allow disabled tenants to make reasonable *modifications* of their living unit at their expense if that is what is needed for the person to comfortably and safely live in the unit. (42 U.S.C. § 3604(f)(3)(A) (1988).) For example, a disabled person has the right to modify his living space to the extent necessary to make the space safe and comfortable, as long as the modifications will not make the unit unacceptable to the next tenant or the disabled tenant agrees to undo the modification when he leaves. Examples of modifications undertaken by a disabled tenant include lowering countertops for a wheelchair-bound tenant.

You are not obliged to allow a disabled tenant to modify his unit at will, without your prior approval. You are entitled to ask for a reasonable description of the proposed modifications, proof that they will be done in a workmanlike manner and evidence that the tenant is obtaining any necessary building permits. Moreover, if a tenant proposes to modify the unit in such a manner that will require restoration when the tenant leaves (such as the repositioning of lowered kitchen counters), you may require that the tenant pay into an interest-bearing escrow account the amount estimated for the restoration. (The interest belongs to the tenant.)

---

or less equally—for example, if you arbitrarily set tougher standards (such as a higher income level or proof of legal status, such as legal papers) for renting to a member of an ethnic minority—you are violating federal laws and opening yourself up to expensive lawsuits and the possibility of being hit with large judgments. On the other hand, if you require *all* prospective tenants to meet the same income standard and to supply satisfactory proof of their legal eligibility to work (as well as meet your other criteria), you will get the needed information, but in a nondiscriminatory way.

⚠️ *Show the property to and accept applications from everyone who's interested.*
Even if, after talking to someone on the phone, you doubt that a particular tenant can qualify, it's best to politely take all applications. Unless you can point to something in writing that clearly disqualifies a tenant, you are always on shaky legal ground. Refusing to take an application may unnecessarily anger a prospective tenant, and may make him or her more likely to look into the possibility of filing a discrimination complaint. Make decisions later about who will rent the property. Be sure to keep copies of all applications. (See discussion of recordkeeping in Chapter 4, Section D.)

F. Choosing—and Rejecting—an Applicant

After you've collected applications and done some screening, you can start sifting through the applicants. Section D, above, covers the basic criteria you need to evaluate when choosing tenants. Start by eliminating the worst risks: people with negative references from previous landlords, a history of nonpayment of rent or poor credit or previous evictions. Then make your selection.

Assuming you choose the best-qualified candidate (based on income, credit history and references), you have no legal problem. But what if you have a number of more or less equally qualified applicants? Can you safely choose an older white man over a young black woman? The answer is a qualified "yes." If two people rate equally, you can legally choose either one without legal risk in any particular situation. But be extra careful not to take the further step of always selecting a person of the same sex, age or ethnicity. For example, if you are a larger landlord who is frequently faced with tough choices and who always avoids an equally qualified minority or disabled applicant, you are guilty of discrimination.

1. Recordkeeping

A crucial use of any tenant-screening system is to document how and why you chose a particular tenant.

Be sure to note your reasons for rejection—such as poor credit history, pets (if you don't accept pets) or a negative reference from a previous landlord—on the Tenant References form or other document so that you have a paper trail if a tenant ever accuses you of illegal discrimination. You want to be able to back up your reason for rejecting the person. Keep organized files of applications, credit reports and other materials and notes on prospective tenants for at least three years after you rent a particular unit. (See the discussion of recordkeeping in Chapter 4, Section D.)

2. Information You Must Provide Rejected Applicants

If you do not rent to someone (or you charge a higher rent) because of an insufficient credit report or negative information in the report, you must give the applicant the name and address of the agency that reported the negative information or furnished the insufficient report. This is a requirement of the federal Fair Credit Report Act. (15 U.S.C. §§ 1681 et. seq.)

You must tell the applicant that he or she has a right to obtain a copy of the file from the agency that reported the negative information, by requesting it within the next 60 days. You must also tell the rejected applicant that the credit reporting agency did not make the decision to reject him as a tenant and cannot explain the reason for the rejection. Finally, you must tell applicants that they can dispute the accuracy of their credit report and add their own consumer statement to their report. The law doesn't require you to communicate an applicant's right to disclosure in writing, but it's a good idea to do so (and to keep a copy of the rejection letter in your files). That way, you'll have irrefutable proof that you complied with the law if you're ever challenged in court. Use the Notice of Denial Based on Credit Report Information form, shown below, to comply with the federal Fair Credit Reporting Act when you reject an applicant because of an insufficient credit report or negative information in the report.

A sample Notice of Denial Based on Credit Report Information form is shown below, and Appendix 2 includes a blank tear-out copy of the form.

Exceptions: The federal requirements do not apply if you reject someone based on other sources, such as information in his application alone or information you obtain from a former landlord.

G. Choosing a Tenant-Manager

Many landlords hire a manager to handle all the day-to-day details of running a rental property, including fielding tenants' routine repair requests and collecting the rent. If you hire a resident manager, make sure he or she (like all other tenants) completes a rental application and that you check references and other information carefully. If you use a property management company, it will do this work for you. (See Section H, below.)

The person you hire as a manager will occupy a critical position in your business. Your manager will interact with every tenant and will often have access to her personal files and her home. Legally, you have a duty to protect your tenants from injuries caused by employees you know (or should know) pose a risk of harm to others. If someone gets hurt or has property stolen or damaged by a manager whose background you didn't check carefully, you could be sued, so it's crucial that you be especially vigilant when hiring a manager.

When you hire a manager, you should sign two separate agreements:

- an employment agreement that covers manager responsibilities, hours and pay that can be terminated at any time for any reason by either party
- a month-to-month rental agreement that can be terminated by either of you with the amount of written notice, typically 30 days, required under state law.

Whether or not you compensate a manager with reduced rent or regular salary, be sure you comply with your legal obligations as an employer, such as following laws governing minimum wage and overtime.

Every Landlord's Legal Guide *by Marcia Stewart, Ralph Warner & Janet Portman (Nolo), provides detailed advice on hiring a manager, including how to prepare a property manager agreement, and your legal obligations as an employer, such as following laws governing minimum wage and overtime.*

The Employer's Legal Handbook, *by Fred S. Steingold (Nolo), is a complete guide to the latest workplace laws and regulations. It covers everything you need to know about hiring and firing employees, personnel policies, employee benefits, discrimination and other laws affecting small business practices.*

H. Property Management Companies

Property management companies are often used by owners of large apartment complexes and by absentee owners too far away from the property to be directly involved in everyday details. Property management companies generally take care of renting units, collecting rent, taking tenant complaints, arranging repairs and maintenance and evicting troublesome tenants. Of course, some of these responsibilities may be shared with or delegated to resident managers who, in some instances, may work for the management company.

A variety of relationships between owners and management companies are possible, depending on your wishes and how the particular management company chooses to do business. For example, if you own one or more big buildings, the management company will probably recommend hiring a resident manager. But if your rental property has only a few units, or you own a number of small buildings spread over a good-sized geographical area, the management company will probably suggest simply responding to tenant requests and complaints from its central office.

One advantage of working with a management company is that you avoid all the legal hassles of being an employer: paying payroll taxes, buying workers' compensation insurance, withholding income tax. The management company is an independent contractor, not an employee. It hires and pays the people who do the work. Typically, you sign a contract spelling out the management company's duties and fees. Most companies charge a fixed percentage—about 5% to 10%—of the total rent

Notice of Denial Based on Credit Report Information

To: _Ryan Paige_
Applicant

1 Mariner Square
Street Address

Seattle, Washington 98101
City, State and Zip Code

THIS NOTICE is to inform you that your application to rent the property at _75 Starbucks Lane, Seattle, WA 98108_

[*rental property address*] has been denied because of [*check all that apply*]:

☒ Insufficient information in the credit report provided by _ABC Credit Bureau, 310 Griffey Way, Seattle, WA 98104, 206-555-1212_

[*name, address and telephone number of consumer credit reporting agency providing credit report; including toll-free telephone number if this is a national credit reporting agency*]

☐ Negative information in the credit report provided by _____

_____

[*name, address and telephone number of consumer credit reporting agency providing credit report; including toll-free telephone number if this is a national credit reporting agency*]

The consumer credit reporting agency noted above did not make the decision not to rent to you and cannot explain why your application was rejected. It only provided information about your credit history.

Providing this notice meets the requirements of the federal Fair Credit Reporting Act (15 U.S.C. §§ 1681 and following). You have the right under this Act to obtain a free copy of your credit report from the consumer credit reporting agency named above, if your request is made within 60 days of this notice (15 U.S.C. § 1681j). You also have the right to dispute the accuracy or completeness of your credit report and add your own "consumer statement" (up to 100 words) to the report (15 U.S.C. § 1681i). For more information, contact the above-named consumer credit reporting agency.

_0-1-0X_   *Jason McGuire*
Date   Owner/Manager

collected. (The salary of any resident manager is additional.) This gives the company a good incentive to keep the building filled with rent-paying tenants.

Another advantage is that management companies are usually well informed about the law, keep good records and are adept at staying out of legal hot water in such areas as discrimination, invasion of privacy and returning deposits.

The primary disadvantage of hiring a management company is the expense. For example, if you pay a management company 10% of the $14,000 you collect in rent each month from tenants in a 20-unit building, this amounts to $1,400 a month and $16,800 per year. While many companies charge less than 10%, it's still quite an expense. Also, if the management company works from a central office with no one on-site, tenants may feel that management is too distant and unconcerned with their day-to-day needs.

Management companies have their own contracts, which you should read thoroughly and understand before signing. Be sure you understand how the company is paid and its exact responsibilities. ■

Getting the Tenant Moved In

Legal disputes between landlords and tenants have gained a reputation for being almost as emotional as divorce court battles. While some may be inevitable, we believe many disputes could be diffused at the start if tenants were better educated as to their legal rights and responsibilities. A clearly written and easy-to-understand lease or rental agreement that details a tenant's obligations and is signed by all adult occupants of your rental unit is the key to starting a tenancy. (See Chapter 2.) But we believe there's more that can be done to help establish a positive relationship when new tenants move in. Most important, you should:

- inspect the property, fill out a Landlord/Tenant Checklist with the tenant and photograph the rental unit
- prepare a move-in letter highlighting important terms of the tenancy and your expectations.

A. Inspect and Photograph the Unit

To eliminate the possibility of all sorts of future arguments, it is absolutely essential that you (or your representative) and prospective tenants (together, if possible) check the place over for damage and obvious wear and tear before the tenant moves in. The best way to document what you find is to jointly fill out a Landlord/Tenant Checklist form and take photographs of the rental unit.

1. Use a Landlord/Tenant Checklist

A Landlord/Tenant Checklist, inventorying the condition of the rental property at the beginning and end of the tenancy, is an excellent device to protect both you and your tenant when the tenant moves out and wants the security deposit returned. Without some record as to the condition of the unit, the tenant is all too likely to make unreasonable demands. For example, is there a landlord alive who has not been falsely told that a stained rug or a cracked mirror or broken stove was already damaged when the tenant moved in?

The checklist provides good evidence as to why you withheld all or part of a security deposit. Coupled with a system to regularly keep track of the rental property's condition, the checklist will also be extremely useful to you if a tenant withholds rent, breaks the lease and moves out or sues you outright, claiming the unit needs substantial repairs.

A sample Landlord/Tenant Checklist is shown below and, Appendix 2 includes a blank tear-out copy of the form.

States That Require A Landlord/Tenant Checklist

The following states require landlords to give new tenants a written statement on the condition of the rental premises at move-in time, including a comprehensive list of existing damages: Arizona, Georgia, Hawaii, Kentucky, Maryland, Massachusetts, Michigan, Montana, North Dakota, Virginia and Washington.

Landlord/Tenant Checklist

GENERAL CONDITION OF ROOMS

572 Fourth St.   Apt. 11   Washington, D.C.
Street Address   Unit Number City

	Condition on Arrival	Condition on Departure	Estimated Cost of Repair/Replacement
LIVING ROOM			
Floors & Floor Coverings	OK		
Drapes & Window Coverings	Mini-blinds discolored		
Walls & Ceilings	OK		
Light Fixtures	OK		
Windows, Screens & Doors	Window rattles		
Front Door & Locks	OK		
Fireplace	N/A		
Other			
Other			
KITCHEN			
Floors & Floor Coverings	Cigarette burn hole		
Walls & Ceilings	OK		
Light Fixtures	OK		
Cabinets	OK		
Counters	Stained		
Stove/Oven	Burners filthy (grease)		
Refrigerator	OK		
Dishwasher	OK		
Garbage Disposal	N/A		
Sink & Plumbing	OK		
Windows, Screens & Doors	OK		
Other			
Other			
DINING ROOM			
Floors & Floor Covering	OK		
Walls & Ceiling	Crack in ceiling		
Light Fixtures	OK		
Windows, Screens & Doors	OK		

	Condition on Arrival	Condition on Departure	Estimated Cost of Repair/Replacement
Other			
Other			
BATHROOM(S)	**Bath 1** **Bath 2**	**Bath 1** **Bath 2**	
Floors & Floor Coverings	OK		
Walls & Ceilings	OK		
Windows, Screens & Doors	OK		
Light Fixtures	OK		
Bathtub/Shower	Tub chipped		
Sink & Counters	OK		
Toilet	Base of toilet very dirty		
Other			
Other			
BEDROOM(S)	**Bdrm 1** **Bdrm 2** **Bdrm 3**	**Bdrm 1** **Bdrm 2** **Bdrm 3**	
Floors & Floor Coverings			
Windows, Screens & Doors	OK OK		
Walls & Ceilings	OK OK		
Light Fixtures	Dented OK		
Other	Mildew in closet		
Other			
OTHER AREAS			
Heating System	OK		
Air Conditioning	OK		
Lawn/Garden	OK		
Stairs & Hallway	N/A		
Patio, Terrace, Deck, etc.	N/A		
Basement	OK		
Parking Area	OK		
Other			
Other			

☒ Tenants acknowledge that all smoke detectors and fire extinguishers were tested in their presence and found to be in working order, and that the testing procedure was explained to them. Tenants agree to test all detectors at least once a month and to report any problems to Landlord/Manager in writing. Tenants agree to replace all smoke detector batteries as necessary.

FURNISHED PROPERTY

	Condition on Arrival	Condition on Departure	Estimated Cost of Repair/Replacement
LIVING ROOM			
Coffee Table	Two scratches on top		
End Tables	OK		
Lamps	OK		
Chairs	OK		
Sofa	OK		
Other			
Other			
KITCHEN			
Broiler Pan	N/A		
Ice Trays	N/A		
Other			
Other			
DINING AREA			
Chairs	OK		
Stools	N/A		
Table	Leg bent slightly		
Other			
Other			
BATHROOM(S)	**Bath 1** **Bath 2**	**Bath 1** **Bath 2**	
Mirrors	OK		
Shower Curtain	Torn		
Hamper	N/A		
Other			
Other			
BEDROOM(S)	**Bdrm 1** **Bdrm 2** **Bdrm 3**	**Bdrm 1** **Bdrm 2** **Bdrm 3**	
Beds (single)	OK N/A		
Beds (double)	N/A OK		
Chairs	OK OK		
Chests	N/A N/A		
Dressing Tables	OK N/A		
Lamps	OK OK		
Mirrors	OK OK		
Night Tables	OK N/A		
Other			
Other			

	Condition on Arrival	Condition on Departure	Estimated Cost of Repair/Replacement
Other			
OTHER AREAS			
Bookcases	N/A		
Desks	N/A		
Pictures	Hallway picture frame chipped		
Other			
Other			

Use this space to provide any additional explanation:

_____

_____

_____

_____

_____

_____

_____

_____

_____

_____

_____

_____

_____

Landlord/Tenant Checklist completed on moving in on _____ May 1 _____, 200 _X_ and approved by:

_Bernard Cohen_____ and _____ _Maria Crouse_____
Landlord/Manager   Tenant

_____ _Sandra Martino_____
                                                             Tenant

_____
                                                             Tenant

Landlord/Tenant Checklist completed on moving out on _____, 200____ and approved by:

_____ and _____
Landlord/Manager   Tenant

_____
                                                             Tenant

_____
                                                             Tenant

2. How to Fill Out the Checklist

You and the tenant should fill out the checklist together. If that's impossible, complete the form and then make a copy and give it to the tenant to review. You should ask the tenant to note any disagreement promptly and return the checklist to you.

The checklist is in two parts. The first side covers the general condition of each room. The second side covers furnishings, such as a living room lamp or bathroom shower curtain. Obviously, you can simply mark "Not Applicable" or "N/A" in most of these boxes if your unit is not furnished or does not have a particular item listed.

If your rental property has rooms or furnishings not listed on the form, note them in the rows labelled "Other," or cross out something that you don't have and write in the changes. If you are renting out a large house or apartment or providing many furnishings, you may want to attach a separate sheet.

In the *Condition on Arrival* column, mark "OK" in the space next to items that are in satisfactory condition. Make a note—as specific as possible—on items that are not working or are dirty, worn, scratched or simply not in the best condition. For example, don't simply note that the refrigerator "needs fixing" if an ice maker doesn't work—it's just as easy to write "ice maker broken, should not be used." This way, if the tenant uses the ice maker anyway and causes water damage in the unit below, he cannot claim that you failed to tell him.

The last two columns—*Condition on Departure* and *Estimated Cost of Repair/Replacement*—are for use when the tenant moves out and, ideally, the two of you inspect the unit again. At that time, the checklist will document your need to make deductions from the security deposit for repairs or cleaning or to replace missing items. (Chapter 5, Section D discusses returning security deposits.) If you don't know what it will cost to fix or replace something, simply write in "Cost will be documented by Landlord."

As part of your move-in procedures, make sure you test all smoke detectors and fire extinguishers in the tenant's presence and show them to be in good working order. Clearly explain to the tenant how to test the smoke detectors and point out the signs—for example, a beeping noise—of a failing detector. Alert tenants to their responsibility to regularly test smoke detectors, and explain how to replace the battery when necessary. Be sure the tenant checks the box on the bottom of the first page of the checklist acknowledging that the smoke detector was tested in his presence and shown to be in working order. By doing this, you'll limit your liability if the smoke detector fails and results in fire damage or injury.

After you and the tenant agree on all of the particulars on the rental unit, you each should sign and date the checklist, as well as any attachments, on both sides. Keep the original for yourself and attach a copy to the tenant's lease or rental agreement. (See Clause 11 of the form agreements in Chapter 2.)

Be sure to keep the checklist up to date if you repair, replace, add or remove items or furnishings after the tenant moves in. Both you and the tenant should initial and date any changes.

3. Photograph the Rental Unit

Taking photos or videotapes of the unit before the tenant moves in is another excellent way to avoid disputes over a tenant's responsibility for damage and dirt. In addition to the checklist, you'll be able to compare "before" and "after" pictures when a tenant leaves. This should help refresh your tenant's memory and may result in her being more reasonable. Certainly, if you end up in mediation or court for not returning the full security deposit, being able to document your point of view with photos will be invaluable. In addition, photos or a video can also help if you have to sue a former tenant for cleaning and repair costs above the deposit amount.

It's best to take "before" photographs with a Polaroid camera that develops pictures on the spot. This will allow both you and the tenant to date and sign the pictures, each keeping a set. Otherwise, use a camera that automatically imprints the date on each photo.

If you make a video, get the tenant on tape saying the date and time so that you can prove when the video was made, and, later, provide him with a copy.

If possible, you should repeat this process after the tenant leaves, as part of your standard move-out procedure. (Chapter 5, Section B discusses how to prepare a move-out letter.)

B. Send New Tenants a Move-In Letter

A move-in letter should dovetail with the lease or rental agreement and provide basic information, such as the manager's phone number and office hours.

You can also use a move-in letter to explain any procedures and rules that are too detailed or numerous to include in your lease or rental agreement. (Alternatively, large landlords may use a set of Rules and Regulations to cover some of these issues. See Clause 18 of the form agreements in Chapter 2.)

Here are some items you may want to cover in a move-in letter:

- how and where to report maintenance and repair problems
- any lock-out or re-key fees
- use of grounds and garage
- your policy regarding rent increases for additional roommates
- location of garbage cans, available recycling programs and trash pickup days
- maintenance do's and don'ts, such as how to avoid overloading circuits and use the garbage disposal properly
- renter's insurance

- other issues, such as pool hours, elevator operation, building access during evening hours and use of a laundry room and storage space, should be covered as needed.

Because every rental situation is at least a little different, we cannot supply you with a generic move-in letter that will work for everyone. We can, however, give you a template for a move-in letter that you can easily fill in with your own details. You can use the sample shown here as a model in preparing your own move-in letter.

We recommend that you make a copy of each tenant's move-in letter for yourself and ask him to sign the last page, indicating that he has read it.

Be sure to update the move-in letter from time to time as necessary.

C. Cash Rent and Security Deposit Checks

Every landlord's nightmare is a new tenant whose first rent or deposit check bounces and who must be dislodged with time-consuming and expensive legal proceedings.

To avoid this, never sign a rental agreement, or let a tenant move furniture into your property or take a key, until you have the tenant's cash, certified check or money order for the first month's rent and security deposit. An alternative is to cash the tenant's check at the bank before the move-in date. (While you have the tenant's first check, photocopy it for your records. The information on it can be helpful if you ever need to sue to collect a judgment from the tenant.) Be sure to give the tenant a signed receipt for the deposit.

Clause 5 of the form lease and rental agreements in Chapter 2 requires tenants to pay rent on the first day of each month. If the move-in date is other than

Move-In Letter

September 1, 200X _____ (date)

Frank O'Hara _____ (tenant)

139 Porter Street _____ (street address)

Madison, Wisconsin 53704 _____ (city and state)

Dear Frank _____, (tenant)

Welcome to ___ Apartment 45 B at Happy Hill Apartments _____

_____ (address of rental unit). We hope you will enjoy living here. This letter is to

explain what you can expect from the management and what we'll be looking for from you:

1. **Rent:** Rent is due on the first of the month. There is no grace period for the payment of rent. (See Clauses 5 and 6 of your rental agreement for details, including late charges.) Also, we don't accept post-dated checks.

2. **New Roommates:** If you want someone to move in as a roommate, please contact us first. If your rental unit is big enough to accommodate another person, we will arrange for the new person to fill out a rental application. If it's approved, all of you will need to sign a new rental agreement. Depending on the situation, there may be a rent increase to add a roommate.

3. **Notice to End Tenancy:** To terminate your month-to-month tenancy, you must give at least 30 days' written notice. We have a written form available for this purpose. We may also terminate the tenancy, or change its terms, on 30 days' written notice. If you give less than 30 days' notice, you will still be financially responsible for rent for the balance of the 30-day period.

4. **Deposits:** Your security deposit will be applied to costs of cleaning, damages or unpaid rent after you move out. You may not apply any part of the deposit toward any part of your rent in the last month of your tenancy. (See Clause 8 of your rental agreement.)

5. **Manager:** Sophie Beauchamp (Apartment #15, phone 555-1234) is your resident manager. You should pay your rent to her and promptly let her know of any maintenance or repair problems (see #7, below) and any other questions or problems. She's in her office every day from 8 a.m. to 10 a.m. and from 4 p.m. to 6 p.m. and can be reached by phone at other times.

6. **Landlord-Tenant Checklist:** By now, Sophie Beauchamp should have taken you on a walk-through of your apartment to check the condition of all walls, drapes, carpets and appliances and to test the smoke alarms and fire extinguisher. These are all listed on the Landlord-Tenant Checklist, which you should have reviewed carefully and signed. When you move out, we will ask you to check each item against its original condition as described on the Checklist.

7. **Maintenance/Repair Problems:** We are determined to maintain a clean, safe building in which all systems are in good repair. To help us make repairs promptly, we will give you Maintenance/Repair Request forms to report to the manager any problems in your apartment, such as a broken garbage disposal, or on the building or grounds, such a burned-out light in the garage. (Extra copies are available from the manager.) In an emergency, or when it's not convenient to use this form, please call the manager at 555-1234.

8. **Semi-Annual Safety and Maintenance Update** To help us keep your unit and the common areas in excellent condition, we'll ask you to fill out a form every six months updating any problems on the premises or in your rental unit. This will allow you to report any potential safety hazards or other problems that otherwise might be overlooked.

9. **Annual Safety Inspection:** Once a year, we will ask to inspect the condition and furnishings of your rental unit and update the Landlord-Tenant Checklist. In keeping with state law, we will give you reasonable notice before the inspection, and you are encouraged to be present for it.

10. **Insurance:** We highly recommend that you purchase renter's insurance. The building property insurance policy will not cover the replacement of your personal belongings if they are lost due to fire, theft or accident. In addition, you could be found liable if someone is injured on the premises you rent as a result of your negligence. If you damage the building itself—for example, if you start a fire in the kitchen and it spreads—you could be responsible for large repair bills.

11. **Moving Out:** It's a little early to bring up moving out, but please be aware that we have a list of items that should be cleaned before we conduct a move-out inspection. If you decide to move, please ask the manager for a copy of our Move-Out Letter explaining our procedures for inspection and returning your deposit.

12. **Telephone Number Changes:** Please notify us if your home or work phone number changes, so we can reach you promptly in an emergency.

Please let us know if you have any questions.

Sincerely,

September 1, 200X   *Tom Guiliano*
Date   Owner

I have read and received a copy of this statement.

September 1, 200X   *Frank O'Hara*
Date   Tenant

the first day of the month, rent is prorated between that day and the end of that month.

D. Organize Your Tenant Records

A good system to record all significant tenant complaints and repair requests will provide a valuable paper trail should disputes develop later—for example, regarding your right to enter a tenant's unit to make repairs, or the time it took for you to fix a problem. Without good records, the outcome of a dispute may come down to your word against your tenant's—always a precarious situation.

Set up a file folder on each property with individual files for each tenant. Include the following documents:

- rental application, references and credit and background information, including information about any cosigners
- a signed lease or rental agreement, plus any changes made along the way
- Landlord-Tenant Checklist and photos or video made at move-in, and
- signed move-in letter.

After a tenant moves in, add these documents to the individual's file:

- your written requests for entry.
- rent increase notices.
- records of repair requests, and details of how and when they were handled. If you keep repair records on the computer, you should regularly print out and save files from past

months; if you have a master system to record all requests and complaints in one log, you would save that log separately, not necessarily put it in every tenant's file.
- safety and maintenance updates and inspection reports, and
- correspondence and other relevant information.

Your computer can also be a valuable tool to keep track of tenants. Set up a simple database for each tenant with spaces for the following information:

- address or unit number
- move-in date
- home phone number
- name, address and phone number of employer
- credit information, including up-to-date information as to where tenant banks
- monthly rent amount and rent due date
- amount and purpose of deposits plus any information your state requires on location of deposit and interest payments
- vehicle make, model, color, year and license plate number
- emergency contacts, and whatever else is important to you.

Once you enter the information into your database, you can sort the list by address or other variables and easily print labels for rent increases or other notices.

If you own many rental properties, you should check into commercial computer programs that allow you to keep track of every aspect of your business, from the tracking of rents to the follow-up on repair requests.

■

Changing or Ending a Tenancy

Sometime after you've signed a lease or rental agreement you may want to make changes—perhaps you need to increase the rent, or you agree to let the tenant bring in a roommate or keep a small pet. This chapter shows how to modify a signed lease or rental agreement. It also discusses how you—or your tenant—may end a tenancy, and offers tips on how to take steps to try and avoid problems, such as a tenant giving inadequate notice and breaking the lease. This chapter also summarizes basic rules for returning security deposits when a tenant leaves.

- *Writing clear lease and rental agreement provisions on notice required to end a tenancy: Chapter 2*
- *How to advertise and rent property before a current tenant leaves: Chapter 3*
- *Highlighting notice requirements in a move-in letter to the tenant: Chapter 4*

A. How to Modify Signed Rental Agreements and Leases

All amendments to your lease or rental agreement should be in writing and signed by both you and the tenant. (Oral changes to oral agreements may be legal, but are a terrible idea.)

If you use a fixed-term lease, you cannot unilaterally alter the terms of the tenancy. For the most part, the lease fixes the terms of the tenancy for the length of the lease. You can't raise the rent or change the terms of the lease until the end of the lease period unless the lease allows it or the tenant agrees. If the tenant agrees to changes, however, simply follow the directions below for amending the rental agreement.

1. Amending a Month-to-Month Rental Agreement

If you want to change one or more clauses in a month-to-month rental agreement, there is no legal requirement that you get the tenant's consent. Legally, you need simply to send the tenant a notice of the change.

Most states require 30 days' advance notice (subject to any rent control ordinances) to change a month-to-month tenancy—for example, to increase the rent. See the "Notice Required to Change or Terminate a Month-to-Month Tenancy" table in Appendix 1 for a list of each state's notice requirements, and Clause 4 of the rental agreement in Chapter 2. You'll need to consult your state statutes for the specific information on how you must deliver a 30-day notice to the tenant. (Most allow you to use first-class mail.)

 Contact the tenant and explain the changes.
It makes good personal and business sense for you or your manager to contact the tenant personally and tell him about a rent increase or other changes before you follow up with a written notice. If the tenant is opposed to your proposal, your personal efforts will allow you to explain your reasons.

You don't generally need to redo the rental agreement in order to make a change or two. Just keep a copy of the change with the rental agreement. In some cases, however, you may want the tenant to sign a new rental agreement—for example, if the tenant initiates a change. If the change is small and simply alters part of an existing clause—such as increasing the rent or making the rent payable every 14 days instead of every 30 days—you can cross out the old language, write in the new and sign in the margin next to the new words. Make sure the tenant also signs next to the change. Be sure to add the date, in case there is a dispute later as to when the change became effective.

Amendment to Lease or Rental Agreement

This is an Amendment to the lease or rental agreement dated _____ March 1, _____ , 200 _X_

(the "Agreement") between _____ Olivia Matthew _____ ("Landlord")

and _____ Steve Phillips _____ ("Tenant")

regarding property located at _____ 1578 Maple St., Seattle _____

_____ ("the premises").

Landlord and Tenant agree to the following changes and/or additions to the Agreement:

1. Beginning on June 1, 200X, Tenant shall rent a one-car garage, adjacent to the main pre-

   mises, from Landlord for the sum of $75 per month.

2. Tenant may keep one German shepherd dog on the premises. The dog shall be kept on a leash

   in the yard unless Tenant is present. Tenant shall clean up all animal waste from the yard on

   a daily basis. Tenant agrees to repair any damages to the yard or premises caused by his

   dog, at Tenant's expense.

_____

_____

_____

_____

_____

May 20, 200X	_Olivia Matthew, Landlord_
Date	Landlord/Landlord's Agent

May 20, 200X	_Steve Phillips, Tenant_
Date	Tenant

Date	Tenant

Date	Tenant

If you do not want to rewrite the entire rental agreement, you can simply add another page, called an "Amendment," to the original document. The amendment should clearly refer to the agreement it's changing and be signed by the same people who signed the original agreement. See the sample, above, which concerns parking and pets.

Appendix 2 includes a blank tear-out version of the Amendment to Lease or Rental Agreement form.

2. Preparing a New Lease or Rental Agreement

If you're adding a clause, or making several changes to your rental agreement, you will probably find it easiest to substitute a whole new agreement for the old one. If you prepare an entire new agreement, be sure that you and the tenant write "Canceled by mutual consent, effective (date)" on the old one, and sign it. In order to avoid the possibility of two inconsistent agreements operating at the same time, be sure that there is no time overlap between the old and new agreements. Similarly, so that the tenant is always subject to a written agreement, do not allow any gap between the cancellation date of the old agreement and the effective date of the new one.

A new tenant should mean a new agreement.
Even if a new tenant is filling out the rest of a former tenant's lease term under the same conditions, it is never wise to allow her to operate under the same lease or rental agreement. Start over and prepare a new agreement in the new tenant's name. (See Clause 10 of the form agreements in Chapter 2.)

B. Ending a Month-to-Month Tenancy

This section discusses a landlord's and a tenant's responsibilities to end a month-to-month tenancy.

1. Giving Notice to the Tenant

If you want a tenant to leave, you can end a month-to-month tenancy simply by giving the proper amount of notice. You don't usually have to state a reason, unless state or local law requires it. In most places, all you need to do is give the tenant a simple written notice that complies with your state's minimum notice requirement and states the date on which the tenancy will end. After that date, the tenant no longer has the legal right to occupy the premises.

In most states, and for most rentals, a landlord who wants to terminate a month-to-month tenancy must provide the same amount of notice as a tenant—typically 30 days. (See Section 2, below.) But this is not true everywhere. For example, in Georgia, landlords must give 60 days' notice to terminate a month-to-month tenancy, while tenants need only give 30 days' notice. (See the "Notice Required to Change or Terminate a Month-to-Month Tenancy" table in Appendix 1.) State and local rent control laws can also impose notice requirements on landlords. Things are different if you want a tenant to move because he or she has violated a material term of the rental agreement—for example, by failing to pay rent. If so, notice requirements are commonly greatly shortened, sometimes to as little as three days.

Each state (and even some cities) has its own very detailed rules and procedures for preparing and serving termination notices, and it is impossible for this book to provide all specific forms and instructions. Consult a landlords' association or local rent control board and your state statutes for information and sample forms. Once you understand how much notice you must give, how the notice must be delivered and any other requirements, you'll be in good shape to handle this work yourself—usually with no lawyer needed.

2. How Much Notice the Tenant Must Give

In most states, the tenant who decides to move out must give you at least 30 days' notice. Some states allow less than 30 days' notice in certain situations—for example, because a tenant must leave early because of military orders or health problems. And, in some states, tenants who pay rent more frequently than once a month can give notice to terminate that matches their rent payment interval—for example, tenants who pay rent every two weeks would have to give 14 days' notice. If your tenant joins the military and wants to terminate a rental agreement, federal law specifies the maximum amount of notice you may require (but if state law requires less notice, you must follow state rules). See sidebar, "Special Rules for Tenants Who Enter Military Service," below.

To educate your tenants as to what they can expect, make sure your rental agreement includes your state's notice requirements for ending a tenancy. (See Clause 4 of the form agreements in Chapter 2.) It is also wise to list termination notice requirements in the move-in letter you send to new tenants. (See Chapter 4, Section B.)

For details on your state's rules, see the "Notice Required to Change or Terminate a Month-to-Month Tenancy" table in Appendix 1.

Restrictions to Ending a Tenancy

The general rules for terminating a tenancy described in this chapter often don't apply in the following situations:

- **Rent control ordinances.** Many rent control cities require "just cause" (a good reason) to end a tenancy, which typically includes moving in a close relative and refurbishing the unit. You will likely have to state your legal reason in the termination notice you give the tenant.

- **Discrimination.** It is illegal to end a tenancy because of a tenant's race, religion or sex; because they have children; or for any other reason constituting illegal discrimination. (Chapter 3, Section E discusses anti-discrimination laws.)

- **Retaliation.** You can not legally terminate a tenancy to retaliate against a tenant for exercising any right under the law, such as the tenant's right to complain to governmental authorities about defective housing conditions or, in many states, to withhold rent because of a health or safety problem the landlord has failed to correct. Chapter 16 of *Every Landlord's Legal Guide*, by Marcia Stewart, Ralph Warner & Janet Portman (Nolo), covers how to avoid tenant retaliation claims.

Special Rules for Tenants Who Enter Military Service

Tenants who enter military service after signing a lease or rental agreement have a federally legislated right to get out of their rental obligations. (*Soldiers' and Sailors' Civil Relief Act of 1940*, 50 App. U.S.C.A. §§ 530 and following.) Tenants must mail written notice of their intent to terminate their tenancy for military reasons to the landlord or manager.

Rental agreements. Once the notice is mailed or delivered, the tenancy will terminate 30 days after the day that rent is next due. For example, if rent is due on the first of June and the tenant mails a notice on May 28, the tenancy will terminate on July 1. This rule takes precedence over any longer notice periods that might be specified in your rental agreement or by state law. If state law or your agreement provides for shorter notice periods, however, the shorter notice will control.

Leases. A tenant who enters military service after signing a lease may terminate the lease by following the procedure for rental agreements, above. For example, suppose a tenant signs a one-year lease in April, agreeing to pay rent on the first of the month. The tenant enlists October 10 and mails you a termination notice on October 11. In this case, you must terminate the tenancy on December 1, 30 days after the first time that rent is due (November 1) following the mailing of the notice. This tenant will have no continuing obligation for rent past December 1, even though this is several months before the lease expires.

3. You Should Insist on a Tenant's Written Notice of Intent to Move

In many states, a tenant's notice must be in writing and give the exact date the tenant plans to move out. Even if it is not required by law, it's a good idea to insist that the tenant give you notice in writing (as does Clause 4 of the form agreements in Chapter 2). Why bother, especially if the tenant politely calls you to say she will be out on a particular date?

Insisting on written notice will prove essential should the tenant not move as planned after you have signed a lease or rental agreement with a new tenant. Not only will this be true if, at the last minute, the tenant tries to claim that he didn't really set a firm move-out date, but it will also be invaluable if a new tenant sues you to recover the costs of temporary housing or storage fees for her belongings because you could not deliver possession of the unit. In turn, you will want to sue the old (holdover) tenant for causing the problem by failing to move out. Should this be necessary, you will have a much stronger case against the holdover tenant if you can produce a written promise to move on a specific date instead of your version of a conversation (which will undoubtedly be disputed by the tenant).

A sample Tenant's Notice of Intent to Move Out form is shown below. Give a copy of this form to any tenant who tells you he or she plans to move.

Appendix 2 at the back of this book includes a blank tear-out copy of the Tenant's Notice of Intent to Move Out.

Tenant's Notice of Intent to Move Out

April 3, 200X _____ (date)

Anne Sakamoto _____ (landlord/manager)

888 Mill Avenue _____ (street address)

Nashville, Tennessee 37126 _____ (city and state)

Dear ___ Ms. Sakamoto _____, (landlord/manager)

This is to notify you that the undersigned tenant(s) ___ Patti and Joe Ellis _____

_____

_____ will be moving from

999 Brook Lane, Apartment Number 11 _____,

on ___ May 3, 200x _____, or

_____ 30 Days _____ from today. This provides at

least ___ 30 Days' _____ written notice as required in our rental agreement.

Sincerely,

Patti Ellis _____
Tenant

Joe Ellis _____
Tenant

_____
Tenant

Chapter 4 explains how a move-in letter can help get a tenancy off to a good start. Similarly, a move-out letter can also help reduce the possibility of disputes, especially over the return of security deposits. Send the letter as soon as you receive notice of the tenant's intent to leave. Your move-out letter should explain the following to the tenant:

- how you expect the rental unit to be left, including specific cleaning requirements
- details on your final inspection procedures and how you will determine what cleaning and damage repair is necessary, requiring a deduction from the tenant's security deposit. (We recommend you check each item on the Landlord/Tenant Checklist described in Chapter 4 and also photograph or videotape the unit when the tenant leaves.)
- what kinds of deposit deductions you may legally make, and
- when and how you will send any refund that is due.

Appendix 2 includes a blank tear-out copy of a Move-Out Letter, and a sample is shown below.

4. Accepting Rent After a 30-Day Notice Is Given

If you accept rent for any period beyond the date the tenant told you he is moving out, this likely cancels the termination notice and creates a new tenancy. An exception would be where a tenant pays you past due rent and you document this in writing.

Suppose, after giving notice, the tenant asks for a little more time in which to move out. Assuming no new tenant is moving in and you are willing to accommodate this request, prepare a written agreement setting out what you have agreed to in detail, and have the tenant sign it. See the sample letter, below, extending the tenant's move-out date.

⚠️ *If you collected the "last month's rent" when the tenant moved in, do not accept rent for the last month of the tenancy.* You are legally obligated to use this money for the last month's rent. Accepting an additional month's rent may extend the tenant's tenancy.

5. When the Tenant Doesn't Give the Required Notice

All too often, a tenant will send or give you a "too short" notice of intent to move. And it's not unheard of for a tenant to move out with no notice or with a wave as he tosses the keys on your doorstep.

A tenant who leaves without giving enough notice has lost the right to occupy the premises but is still obligated to pay rent through the end of the required notice period. For example, if the notice period is 30 days, but the tenant moves out after telling you 20 days ago that he intended to move, he still owes you rent for the remaining 10 days.

In most states, you have a legal duty to try to re-rent the property before you can charge the tenant for giving you too little notice, but few courts expect a landlord to accomplish this in less than a month. (This rule, called the landlord's duty to mitigate damages, is discussed in Section C4, below.) You can also use the security deposit to cover unpaid rent, as discussed in Section D1, below.

Move-Out Letter

July 5, 200X _____ (date)

Jane Wasserman _____ (tenant)

123 North Street, Apartment #23 _____ (street address)

Atlanta, Georgia 30360 _____ (city and state)

Dear Jane _____ (tenant)

We hope you have enjoyed living here. In order that we may mutually end our relationship on a positive note, this move-out letter describes how we expect your unit to be left and what our procedures are for returning your security deposit.

Basically, we expect you to leave your rental unit in the same condition it was when you moved in, except for normal wear and tear. To refresh your memory on the condition of the unit when you moved in, I've attached a copy of the Landlord/Tenant Checklist you signed at the beginning of your tenancy. I'll be using this same form to inspect your unit when you leave.

Specifically, here's a list of items you should thoroughly clean before vacating:

- ☑ Floors
    - ☑ sweep wood floors
    - ☑ vacuum carpets and rugs (shampoo if necessary)
    - ☑ mop kitchen and bathroom floors
- ☑ Walls, baseboards, ceilings and built-in shelves
- ☑ Kitchen cabinets, countertops and sink, stove and oven—inside and out
- ☑ Refrigerator—clean inside and out, empty it of food and turn it off
- ☑ Bathtubs, showers, toilets and plumbing fixtures
- ☑ Doors, windows and window coverings
- ☑ Other _clean microwave oven—inside and out_

_____

_____

_____

_____

_____

_____

If you have any questions as to the type of cleaning we expect, please let me know.

Please don't leave _anything_ behind—that includes bags of garbage, clothes, food, newspapers, furniture, appliances, dishes, plants, cleaning supplies or other items that belong to you.

Please be sure you have disconnected phone and utility services, canceled all newspaper subscriptions and sent the post office a change-of-address form.

Once you have cleaned your unit and removed _all_ your belongings, please call me at _____555-1234_____ to arrange for a walk-through inspection and to return all keys. Please be prepared to give me your forwarding address where we may mail your security deposit.

It's our policy to return all deposits either in person or at an address you provide within _____one month_____ after you move out. If any deductions are made—for past due rent or because the unit is damaged or not sufficiently clean—they will be explained in writing.

If you have any questions, please contact me at _____555-1234_____.

Sincerely,

Denise Parsons
Landlord/Manager

6. When You or Your Tenant Violates the Rental Agreement

If you seriously violate the rental agreement and fail to fulfill your legal responsibilities—for example, by not correcting serious health or safety problems—a tenant may be able to legally move out with no written notice or by giving less notice than is otherwise required. Called a "constructive eviction," this doctrine typically applies only when living conditions are intolerable—for example, if the tenant has had no heat for an extended period in the winter, or if a tenant's use and enjoyment of the property has been substantially impaired because of drug dealing in the building.

What exactly constitutes a constructive eviction varies slightly under the laws of different states. Generally, if you are on notice that a rental unit has serious habitability problems for an extended time, the tenant is entitled to move out on short notice or, in extreme cases, without giving notice.

Along the same lines, a landlord may evict a tenant who violates a lease or rental agreement. For example, you may give a "notice to quit" to a tenant who fails to pay rent or damages the premises, with less notice than is normally required to end a tenancy (typically three to five days, rather than 30 days). And, in the case of drug dealing, many states provide for expedited eviction procedures. Because of the wide state-by-state variations on eviction rules and procedures, the details of how to evict a tenant are beyond the scope of this book.

C. How Fixed-Term Leases End

A lease lasts for a fixed term, typically one year. As a general rule, neither you nor the tenant may unilaterally terminate the tenancy or change a material condition during the period of the lease, unless the other party has violated the terms of the lease. (There's an exception for tenants who join the military and want to terminate a lease, as explained in the sidebar, "Special Rules for Tenants Who Enter Military Service," above.)

If you and the tenant both live up to your promises, the lease simply ends of its own accord at the end of the lease term, and the tenant moves out. Alternatively, you may sign a new lease, with the same or different terms. As every landlord knows, however, life is not always so simple. Sooner or later, a tenant will stay beyond the end of the term without signing a new lease, or leave before the lease term ends without any legal right to do so.

1. Giving Notice to the Tenant

Because a lease clearly states when it will expire, you may not think it's necessary to remind the tenants of the expiration date. But doing so is a very good practice, and some states or cities (especially those with rent control) actually require it.

We suggest giving the tenant at least 60 days' written notice that the lease is going to expire. This reminder has several advantages:

- **Getting the tenant out on time.** Two months' notice allows plenty of time for the tenant to look for another place if he doesn't —or you don't—want to renew the lease.
- **Giving you time to renegotiate the lease.** If you would like to continue renting to your present tenant but also want to change some lease terms or increase the rent, your notice serves to remind the tenant that the terms of the old lease will not automatically continue. Encourage the tenant to stay, but mention that you need to make some changes to the lease.
- **Getting a new tenant in quickly.** If you know a tenant is going to move, you can show the unit to prospective tenants ahead of time and minimize the time the space is vacant. You must still respect the current tenant's privacy. (Chapter 3, Section B discusses showing the unit to prospective tenants.)

Sample Letter Extending Tenant's Move-Out Date

June 20, 200X

Hannah Lewis
777 Broadway Terrace, Apartment #3
Richmond, Virginia 23233

Dear Hannah:

On June 1, you gave me a 30-day notice of your intent to move out on July 1. You have since requested to extend your move-out to July 18 because of last-minute problems with closing escrow on your new house. This letter is to verify our understanding that you will move out on July 18, instead of July 1, and that you will pay prorated rent for 18 days (July 1 through July 18). Prorated rent for 18 days, based on your monthly rent of $900 or $30 per day, is $540.

Please sign below to indicate your agreement to these terms.

Sincerely,

Fran Moore, Landlord

Agreed to by Hannah Lewis, Tenant:
Signature *Hannah Lewis*
Date *June 20, 200X*

⌂$ ***Your options may be limited in a rent control area.***

If your property is subject to rent control, you may be limited in your ability to end your relationship with a current tenant. Many ordinances require "just cause" for refusing to renew a lease, which generally means that only certain reasons (such as the tenant's failure to pay rent, or your desire to move in a close relative) justify nonrenewal. If your city requires "just cause," and if your decision not to renew does not meet the city's test, you may end up with a perpetual month-to-month tenant. Check your city's rent control ordinance carefully.

2. If the Tenant Remains After the Lease Expires

It's fairly common for a tenant to remain in a unit even though the lease has run out. If this happens, you have a choice: You can continue renting to the tenant, or you can take legal steps to get the tenant out.

If a tenant stays beyond the end of the lease, and you accept rent money without signing a new lease, in most states you will have created a new, month-to-month tenancy on the same terms as applied for the old lease. In a few states, you may create a new lease for the same term—such as one year. In other words, you'll be stuck with the terms and rent in the old lease, at least for the first 30 days and possibly longer. If you want to change the terms in a new lease, you must abide by the law regarding giving notice for a month-to-month tenancy (see Section B, above). It will usually take you at least a month while you go about giving notice to your now month-to-month tenant.

To avoid problems of tenants staying longer than you want, be sure to notify the tenant that you expect him to leave at the lease expiration date, and don't accept rent after this date. If a tenant just wants to stay an extra few days after a lease expires and you agree, it is wise to put your understanding on this arrangement in a letter. (See the sample letter extending the tenant's move-out date, above.)

3. If the Tenant Leaves Early

A tenant who leaves (with or without notifying you beforehand) before a fixed-term lease expires and refuses to pay the remainder of the rent due under the lease is said to have "broken the lease." Once the tenant leaves for good, you have the legal right to take possession of the premises and re-rent to another tenant.

A key question that arises is, how much does a tenant with a lease owe if she walks out early? Let's start with the general legal rule. A tenant who signs a lease agrees at the outset to pay a fixed amount of rent: the monthly rent multiplied by the number of months of the lease. The tenant is obligated to pay this amount in monthly installments over the term of the lease. The fact that payments are made monthly doesn't change the tenant's responsibility to pay rent for the entire lease term. And the fact that a tenant who breaks a lease gives you notice of her intention to leave early changes nothing—you are still owed the money for the rest of the term. As discussed below, depending on the situation, you may use the tenant's security deposit to cover part of the shortfall, or sue the tenant for rent owed.

💡 ***Require tenants to notify you of extended absences.***

Clause 16 of the form lease and rental agreements (Chapter 2) requires tenants to inform you when they will be gone for an extended time, such as two or more weeks.

By requiring tenants to notify you of long absences, you'll know whether property has been abandoned or the tenant is simply on vacation. In addition, if you have such a clause and, under its authority, enter an apparently abandoned unit only to be confronted later by an indignant tenant, you can defend yourself by pointing out that the tenant violated the lease.

When Leaving Early Is Justified

There are some important exceptions to the blanket rule that a tenant who breaks a lease owes you the rent for the entire lease term. A tenant who leaves early may *not* owe if:

- **Your rental unit is unsafe or otherwise uninhabitable.** If you don't live up to your obligations to provide habitable housing—for example, if you fail to maintain the unit in accordance with health and safety codes—a court will conclude that you have "constructively evicted" the tenant. That releases the tenant from further obligations under the lease. (Section B6, above, discusses constructive evictions.)

- **You have rented—or could rent—the unit to someone else.** Most courts require landlords to try to soften ("mitigate") the extenant's liability for the remaining rent by attempting to find a new rent-paying tenant as soon as possible. The new tenant's rent is credited against what the former tenant owed. (Because this "mitigation of damages" rule can be so important, Section C4, below, looks at it in more detail.)

- **State law allows the tenant to leave early.** A few states have laws that list allowable reasons to break a lease. For example,

in Delaware, a tenant need only give 30 days' notice to end a long-term lease if he needs to move because his present employer relocated or because health problems (of the tenant or a family member) require a permanent move. Some states, such as Georgia, allow members of the military to break a lease because of a change in military orders. If your tenant has a good reason for a sudden move, you may want to research your state's law to see whether or not he's still on the hook for rent.

- **The rental unit is damaged or destroyed.** If a tenant's home is significantly damaged—either by natural disaster or any other reason beyond his control—he has the right to consider the lease at an end and to move out. State laws vary on the extent of the landlord's responsibility, depending on the cause of the damage. If a fire, flood, tornado, earthquake or other natural disaster makes the dwelling unlivable, or if a third party is the cause of the destruction (for instance, a fire due to an arsonist), your best bet is to look to your insurance policy for help in repairing or rebuilding the unit and to assist your tenants in resettlement.

4. Your Duty to Mitigate Your Loss If the Tenant Leaves Early

If a tenant breaks the lease and moves out without legal justification, you can't just sit back and wait until the end of the term of the lease, and then sue the departed tenant for the total amount of your lost rent. In most states, you must try to re-rent the property reasonably quickly and subtract the rent you receive from the amount the original tenant owed you.

Even if this isn't the legal rule in your state, trying to re-rent is obviously a sound business strategy. It's much better to have rent coming in every month than to wait, leaving a rental unit vacant for months, and then try to sue (and collect from) a tenant who may be long gone, broke or otherwise difficult to collect from.

If you don't make an attempt (or make an inadequate one) to re-rent, and instead sue the former tenant for the whole rent, you will collect only what the judge thinks is the difference between the fair rental value of the property had you re-rented it and the original tenant's promised rent. This can depend on how easy it is to re-rent in your area. Also, a judge is sure to give you some time (probably at least 30 days) to find a new tenant.

5. How to Mitigate Your Damages

When you're sure that a tenant has left permanently, then you can turn your attention to re-renting the unit.

You do not need to relax your standards for acceptable tenants—for example, you are entitled to reject applicants with poor credit or rental histories. Also, you need not give the suddenly available property priority over other rental units that you would normally attend to first.

You are not required to rent the premises at a rate substantially below its fair market value. Keep in mind, however, that refusing to rent at less than the original rate may be foolish. If you are unable

to ultimately collect from the former tenant, you will get *no* income from the property instead of less. You will have ended up hurting no one but yourself.

Keep Good Records

If you end up suing a former tenant, you will want to be able to show the judge that you acted reasonably in your attempts to re-rent the property. Don't rely on your memory and powers of persuasion to convince the judge. Keep detailed records, including:

- the original lease
- receipts for cleaning and painting, with photos of the unit showing the need for repairs, if any
- your expenses for storing or properly disposing of any belongings the tenant left
- receipts for advertising the property and bills from credit reporting agencies investigating potential renters
- a log of the time you spent showing the property, and the value of that time
- a log of any people who offered to rent and, if you rejected them, documentation as to why, and
- if the current rent is less than that the original tenant paid, a copy of the new lease.

6. The Tenant's Right to Find a Replacement Tenant

A tenant who wishes to leave before the lease expires may offer to find a suitable new tenant, so that the flow of rent will remain uninterrupted, and he will be off the hook for future rent payments. Unless you have a new tenant waiting, you have nothing to lose by cooperating. And refusing to co-operate could hurt you: If you refuse to accept an excellent new tenant and then withhold the lease-breaking tenant's deposit or sue for unpaid rent, you may wind up losing in court since, after all, you turned down the chance to reduce your losses (mitigate your damages).

Of course, if the rental market is really tight in your area, you may be able to lease the unit easily at a higher rent, or you may already have an even better prospective tenant on your waiting list. In that case, you won't care if a tenant breaks the lease, and you may not be interested in any new tenant he provides.

If you and the outgoing tenant agree on a re-placement tenant, you and the new tenant should sign a new lease.

7. When You Can Sue

If a tenant leaves prematurely, you may need to go to court and sue for your re-rental costs and the difference between the original and the replacement rent. (Obviously, you should first use the tenant's deposit, if possible, to cover these costs. See Section D, below.)

Deciding *where* to sue is usually easy: Small claims court is usually the court of choice, because it's fast and affordable and doesn't require a lawyer. The only exception is in states where small claims courts have very low dollar limits and you are owed lots more.

Knowing *when* to sue is trickier. You may be eager to start legal proceedings as soon as the original tenant leaves, but, if you do, you won't know the extent of your losses, because you might find another tenant who will make up part of the lost rent. Must you wait until the end of the original tenant's lease? Or can you bring suit when you re-rent the property?

The standard approach, and one that all states allow, is to go to court after you re-rent the property. At this point, your losses—your expenses and the rent differential, if any—are known and final. The

disadvantage is that you have had no income from that property since the original tenant left, and the original tenant may be long gone and not, practically speaking, worth chasing down.

Nolo's Book on Small Claims Court

Everybody's Guide to Small Claims Court (National Edition), by Ralph Warner (Nolo), provides detailed advice on bringing or defending a small claims court case, preparing evidence and witnesses for court and collecting your court judgment when you win. *Everybody's Guide to Small Claims Court* will also be useful in defending yourself against a tenant who sues you in small claims court—for example, claiming that you failed to return a cleaning or security deposit.

D. Returning Security Deposits When a Tenancy Ends

Most states set very specific rules for the return of security deposits when a tenant leaves—whether voluntarily or by your ending the tenancy. A landlord's failure to return security deposits as legally required can result in substantial financial penalties if a tenant files suit.

1. Basic Rules for Returning Deposits

You are generally entitled to deduct from a tenant's security deposit whatever amount you need to fix damaged or dirty property (outside of "ordinary wear and tear") or to make up unpaid rent. But you must make your deductions and return deposits correctly. While the specific rules vary from state to state, you usually have between 14 and 30 days after the tenant leaves to return the deposit. (See "State Security Deposit Rules" in Appendix 1.)

State security deposit statutes typically require you to mail the following within the time limit to the tenant's last known address (or forwarding address if you have one):

- The tenant's entire deposit with interest if required (see "States That Require Landlords to Pay Interest on Deposits" in Appendix 1).
- A written itemized accounting of deductions, including back rent and costs of cleaning and damage repair, together with payment for any deposit balance. The statement should list each deduction and briefly explain what it's for.

Even if there is no specific time limit in your state or law requiring itemization, promptly presenting the tenant with a written itemization of all deductions and a clear reason why each was made is an essential part of a savvy landlord's overall plan to avoid disputes with tenants. In general, we recommend three to four weeks as a reasonable time.

2. Penalties for Violating Security Deposit Laws

If you don't follow state security deposit laws to the letter, you may pay a heavy price if a tenant sues you and wins. In addition to whatever amount you wrongfully withheld, you may have to pay the tenant extra or punitive damages (penalties imposed when the judge feels that the defendant has acted especially outrageously) and court costs. In many states, if you "willfully" (deliberately and not through inadvertence) violate the security deposit statute, you may forfeit your right to retain any part of the deposit and may be liable for two or three times the amount wrongfully withheld, plus attorney fees and costs.

3. If the Deposit Doesn't Cover Damage and Unpaid Rent

If the security deposit doesn't cover what a tenant owes you, you may wish to file a small claims lawsuit against the former tenant.

Every Landlord's Legal Guide, *by Marcia Stewart, Ralph Warner & Janet Portman (Nolo) provides complete details on state laws and sample forms for returning and itemizing security deposits.*

State Landlord-Tenant Law Charts

Where to Find Landlord-Tenant Laws

Every landlord is governed by state, local and federal law. If you're a typical landlord, you'll primarily be concerned with state law. Citations for state laws on important subjects such as security deposit rules are provided in this Appendix. Most states have made their statutes available online. You can find these by going to Nolo's website at www.nolo.com. Click under "Legal Research Center" where it says "State Laws." Then click on the name of your state to find a particular statute. You can also access federal laws and regulations at Nolo's Legal Research Center. If you are looking for a local ordinance, for example, rent control rules or health and safety standards that affect landlords, check out State and Local Government on the Net (formerly PiperInfo) at www.statelocalgov.net. This is an excellent source for finding local governments online. First click your state, then scroll down the page to find your local government's site.

State Landlord-Tenant Statutes

Here are some of the key statutes pertaining to landlord-tenant law in each state. In some states, important legal principles are contained in court opinions, not codes or statutes. Court-made law is not reflected in this chart.

State	Statute	State	Statute
Alabama	Ala. Code §§ 35-9-1 to 35-9-100	Montana	Mont. Code Ann. §§ 70-24-101 to 70-25-206
Alaska	Alaska Stat. §§ 34.03.010 to 34.03.380	Nebraska	Neb. Rev. Stat. §§ 76-1401 to 76-1449
Arizona	Ariz. Rev. Stat. Ann. §§ 12-1171 to 12-1183, §§ 33-1301 to 33-1381	Nevada	Nev. Rev. Stat. Ann. §§ 118A.010 to 118A.520
Arkansas	Ark. Code Ann. §§ 18-16-101 to 18-16-306	New Hampshire	N.H. Rev. Stat. Ann. §§ 540:1 to 540:29, 540-A:1 to 540-A:8
California	Cal. Civ. Code §§ 1925 to 1954, 1961 to 1962.7, 1995.010 to 1997.270	New Jersey	N.J. Stat. Ann. §§ 46:8-1 to 46:8-49
Colorado	Colo. Rev. Stat. §§ 38-12-101 to 38-12-104, 38-12-301 to 38-12-302	New Mexico	N.M. Stat. Ann. §§ 47-8-1 to 47-8-51
Connecticut	Conn. Gen. Stat. Ann. §§ 47a-1 to 47a-51	New York	N.Y. Real Prop. Law §§ 220 to 238, Real Prop. Acts. §§ 701 to 853, Mult. Dwell. Law (all), Mult. Res. Law (all), Gen. Oblig. Law §§ 7-103 to 7-108
Delaware	Del. Code Ann. tit. 25, §§ 5101 to 7013	North Carolina	N.C. Gen. Stat. §§ 42-1 to 42-14.2, 42-25.6 to 42-76
Dist. of Columbia	D.C. Code Ann. §§ 42-3201 to 42-3610	North Dakota	N.D. Cent. Code §§ 47-16-01 to 47-16-41
Florida	Fla. Stat. Ann. §§ 83.40 to 83.66	Ohio	Ohio Rev. Code Ann. §§ 5321.01 to 5321.19
Georgia	Ga. Code Ann. §§ 44-7-1 to 44-7-81	Oklahoma	Okla. Stat. Ann. tit. 41, §§ 1 to 136
Hawaii	Haw. Rev. Stat. §§ 521-1 to 521-78	Oregon	Or. Rev. Stat. §§ 90.100 to 90.450
Idaho	Idaho Code §§ 6-301 to 6-324, §§ 55-208 to 55-308	Pennsylvania	68 Pa. Cons. Stat. Ann. §§ 250.101 to 250.510-B
Illinois	765 Ill. Comp. Stat. §§ 705/0.01 to 740/5	Rhode Island	R.I. Gen. Laws §§ 34-18-1 to 34-18-57
Indiana	Ind. Code Ann. §§ 32-31-1-1 to 32-31-8-6	South Carolina	S.C. Code Ann. §§ 27-40-10 to 27-40-910
Iowa	Iowa Code Ann. §§ 562A.1 to 562A.36	South Dakota	S.D. Codified Laws Ann. §§ 43-32-1 to 43-32-29
Kansas	Kan. Stat. Ann. §§ 58-2501 to 58-2573	Tennessee	Tenn. Code Ann. §§ 66-28-101 to 66-28-520
Kentucky	Ky. Rev. Stat. Ann. §§ 383.010 to 383.715	Texas	Tex. Prop. Code Ann. §§ 91.001 to 92.354
Louisiana	La. Rev. Stat. Ann. §§ 9:3201 to 9:3259; La. Civ. Code Ann. art. 2669 to 2742	Utah	Utah Code Ann. §§ 57-17-1 to 57-17-5, 57-22-1 to 57-22-6
Maine	Me. Rev. Stat. Ann. tit. 14, §§ 6001 to 6046	Vermont	Vt. Stat. Ann. tit. 9, §§ 4451 to 4468
Maryland	Md. Code Ann. [Real Prop.] §§ 8-101 to 8-604	Virginia	Va. Code Ann. §§ 55-218.1 to 55-248.40
Massachusetts	Mass. Gen. Laws Ann. ch. 186, §§ 1 to 21	Washington	Wash. Rev. Code Ann. §§ 59.04.010 to 59.04.900, 59.18.010 to 59.18.911
Michigan	Mich. Comp. Laws §§ 554.601 to 554.640	West Virginia	W. Va. Code §§ 37-6-1 to 37-6-30
Minnesota	Minn. Stat. Ann. §§ 504B.001 to 504B.471	Wisconsin	Wis. Stat. Ann. §§ 704.01 to 704.50
Mississippi	Miss. Code Ann. §§ 89-8-1 to 89-8-27	Wyoming	Wyo. Stat. §§ 1-21-1201 to 1-21-1211, §§ 34-2-128 to 34-2-129
Missouri	Mo. Rev. Stat. §§ 441.005 to 441.880, §§ 535.150 to 535.300		

Notice Required to Change or Terminate a Month-to-Month Tenancy

Except where noted, the amount of notice a landlord must give to increase rent or change another term of the rental agreement in month-to-month tenancy is the same as that required to end a month-to-month tenancy. Be sure to check state and local rent control laws, which may have different notice requirements.

State	Tenant	Landlord	Statute	Comments
Alabama	10 days	10 days	Ala. Code § 35-9-3	No state statute on the amount of notice required to change rent or other terms.
Alaska	30 days	30 days	Alaska Stat. § 34.03.290(b)	
Arizona	30 days	30 days	Ariz. Rev. Stat. Ann. § 33-1375	
Arkansas	10 days	10 days	Ark. Code Ann. § 18-16-101	
California	30 days	30 or 60 days	Cal. Civ. Code § 1946; Cal. Civ. Code §§ 827a, 827b	Landlord and tenant may agree to a shorter termination notice period, but not less than seven days. If landlord is raising the rent, tenant gets 60 days' notice if the sum of this and all prior rent increases during the previous 12 months is more than 10% of the lowest rent charged during that time. Tenants in Los Angeles, Santa Monica and West Hollywood are entitled to 60 days' notice.
Colorado			No statute	
Connecticut			No statute	
Delaware	60 days	60 days	Del. Code Ann. tit. 25, §§ 5106 and 5107	After receiving notice of landlord's proposed change terms, tenant has 15 days to terminate tenancy. Otherwise, changes will take effect as announced.
District of Columbia	30 days	30 days	D.C. Code Ann. § 42-3202	No state statute on the amount of notice required to change rent or other terms.
Florida	15 days	15 days	Fla. Stat. Ann. § 83.57	No state statute on the amount of notice required to change rent or other terms.
Georgia	30 days	60 days	Ga. Code Ann. § 44-7-7	No state statute on the amount of notice required to change rent or other terms.
Hawaii	28 days	45 days	Haw. Rev. Stat. §§ 521-71 and 521-21(d)	
Idaho	One month	One month	Idaho Code §§ 55-208 and 55-307	Landlords must provide 15 days' notice to increase rent or change tenancy.
Illinois	30 days	30 days	735 Ill. Comp. Stat. 5/9-207	
Indiana	One month	One month	Ind. Code Ann. § 32-31-1-1	
Iowa	30 days	30 days	Iowa Code Ann. §§ 562A.34, 562A.13(5)	
Kansas	30 days	30 days	Kan. Stat. Ann. § 58-2570	No state statute on the amount of notice required to change rent or other terms.
Kentucky	30 days	30 days	Ky. Rev. Stat. Ann. § 383.695	
Louisiana	10 days	10 days	La. Civ. Code Art. 2686	No state statute on the amount of notice required to change rent or other terms.
Maine	30 days	30 days	Me. Rev. Stat. Ann. tit. 14 § 6002	
Maryland	One month	One month	Md. Code Ann. [Real Prop.] § 8-402(b)(3), (4)	Two months notice required in Montgomery County. Does not apply in Baltimore.
Massachusetts	See 1 below	See 1 below	Mass. Gen. Laws Ann. ch. 186 § 12	
Michigan	See 2 below	See 2 below	Mich. Comp. Laws § 554.134	No state statute on the amount of notice required to change rent or other terms.
Minnesota	See 3 below	See 3 below	Minn. Stat. Ann. § 504B.135	No state statute on the amount of notice required to change rent or other terms.
Mississippi	30 days	30 days	Miss. Code Ann. § 89-8-19	No state statute on the amount of notice required to change rent or other terms.

1. Interval between days of payment or 30 days, whichever is longer.
2. Interval between times of payment.
3. Interval between time rent is due.

Notice Required to Change or Terminate a Month-to-Month Tenancy (continued)

State	Tenant	Landlord	Statute	Comments
Missouri	One month	One month	Mo. Rev. Stat. § 441.060	No state statute on the amount of notice required to change rent or other terms.
Montana	30 days	30 days	Mont. Code Ann. § 70-24-441	No state statute on the amount of notice required to change rent or other terms.
Nebraska	30 days	30 days	Neb. Rev. Stat. § 76-1437	No state statute on the amount of notice required to change rent or other terms.
Nevada	30 days	30 days	Nev. Rev. Stat. Ann. §§ 40.251, 118A.300	Landlords must provide 45 days' notice to increase rent.
New Hampshire	30 days	30 days	N.H. Rev. Stat. Ann. §§ 540:2 and 540:3	Landlord may terminate only for just cause.
New Jersey			No statute	
New Mexico	30 days	30 days	N.M. Stat. Ann. §§ 47-8-37, 47-8-15(F)	Landlord must deliver rent increase notice at least 30 days before rent due date.
New York	One month	One month	N.Y. Real Prop. Law § 232-b	No state statute on the amount of notice required to change rent or other terms.
North Carolina	7 days	7 days	N.C. Gen. Stat. § 42-14	No state statute on the amount of notice required to change rent or other terms.
North Dakota	30 days	30 days	N.D. Cent. Code § 47-16-15	Tenant may terminate with 25 days' notice if landlord has changed the terms of the lease.
Ohio	30 days	30 days	Ohio Rev. Code Ann. § 5321.17	No state statute on the amount of notice required to change rent or other terms.
Oklahoma	30 days	30 days	Okla. Stat. Ann. tit. 41, § 111	No state statute on the amount of notice required to change rent or other terms.
Oregon	30 days	30 days	Or. Rev. Stat. § 91.070	
Pennsylvania			No statute	
Rhode Island	30 days	30 days	R.I. Gen. Laws §§ 34-18-16.1 and 34-18-37	
South Carolina	30 days	30 days	S.C. Code Ann. § 27-40-770	No state statute on the amount of notice required to change rent or other terms.
South Dakota	One month	One month	S.D. Codified Laws Ann. §§ 43-32-13 and 43-8-8	Tenant may terminate within 15 days of receiving landlord's modification notice.
Tennessee	30 days	30 days	Tenn. Code Ann. § 66-28-512	No state statute on the amount of notice required to change rent or other terms.
Texas	One month	One month	Tex. Prop. Code Ann. § 91.001	No state statute on the amount of notice required to change rent or other terms.
Utah			No statute	
Vermont	One rental period	30 days	Vt. Code Ann. tit. 9, §§ 4467 and 4456(d)	If there is no written rental agreement, for tenants who have continuously resided in the unit for two years or less, 60 days' notice to terminate; for those who have resided longer than two years, 90 days. If there is a written rental agreement, for tenants who have lived continuously in the unit for two years or less, 30 days; for those who have lived there longer than two years, 60 days.
Virginia	30 days	30 days	Va. Code Ann. §§ 55-248.37 and 55-248.7	No state statute on the amount of notice required to change rent or other terms, but landlord must abide by notice provisions in the rental agreement, if any, and tenant must consent in writing to any change.
Washington	30 days	20 days	Wash. Rev. Code Ann. §§ 59.18.200, 59.18.140	Landlord must give 30 days to change rent or other lease terms.
West Virginia	One month	One month	W. Va. Code § 37-6-5	No state statute on the amount of notice required to change rent or other terms.
Wisconsin	28 days	28 days	Wis. Stat. Ann. § 704.19	No state statute on the amount of notice required to change rent or other terms.
Wyoming			No statute	

State Rent Rules

Here are citations for statues that set out rent rules in each state. When a state has no statute, the space is left blank. See the "Notice Required to Change or Terminate a Month-to-Month Tenancy" chart in this Appendix for citations to raising rent.

State	When Rent Is Due	Grace Period	Where Rent Is Due	Late Fees
Alabama				
Alaska	Alaska Stat. § 34.03.020(c)		Alaska Stat. § 34.03.020(c)	
Arizona	Ariz. Rev. Stat. Ann. §§ 33-1314(C), 33-1368(B)		Ariz. Rev. Stat. Ann. § 33-1314(C)	Ariz. Rev. Stat. Ann. § 33-1368(B)
Arkansas				
California	Cal. Civil Code § 1947		Cal. Civil Code § 1962	*Jack v. Sinsheimer*, 125 C563 (1899); *Ricker v. Rombough*, 120 Cal. App. 2d Supp. 912 (1953), but see *Canal-Randolph Anaheim, Inc. v. Wilcowski*, 78 Cal. App. 3d 477 (1978) [1]
Colorado				
Connecticut	Conn. Gen. Stat. Ann. § 47a-3a	Conn. Gen. Stat. Ann. § 47a-15a	Conn. Gen. Stat. Ann. § 47a-3a	Conn. Gen. Stat. Ann. §§ 47a-4(a)(8), 47a-15a [2]
Delaware	Del. Code Ann. tit. 25, § 5501(b)	Del. Code Ann. tit. 25, § 5501(d)	Del. Code Ann. title 25, § 5501(b)	Del. Code Ann. tit. 25, § 5501(d) [3]
D.C.				
Florida	Fla. Stat. Ann. § 83.46			
Georgia				
Hawaii	Haw. Rev. Stat. § 521-21(b)		Haw. Rev. Stat. § 521-21(b)	
Idaho				
Illinois				
Indiana	*Watson v. Penn,* 108 Ind. 21 (1886), 8 N.E. 636 (1886)			
Iowa	Iowa Code Ann. § 562A.9(3)		Iowa Code Ann. § 562A.9(3)	Iowa Code Ann. § 535.2(7) [4]
Kansas	Kan. Stat. Ann. § 58-2545		Kan. Stat. Ann. § 58-2545	
Kentucky	Ky. Rev. Stat. Ann. § 383.565(2)		Ky. Rev. Stat. Ann. § 383.565(2)	
Louisiana				
Maine		Me. Rev. Stat. Ann. tit. 14, § 6028		Me. Rev. Stat. Ann. tit. 14, § 6028 [5]
Maryland				Md. Code Ann. [Real Prop.] § 8-208(d)(3) [6]
Massachusetts		Mass. Gen. Laws Ann. ch. 186 § 15B(1)(c)		Mass. Gen. Laws Ann. ch. 186 § 15B(1)(c) [7]

[1] Technically, under old but valid California case law, preset late fees are unenforceable, but landlords who set a reasonable fee—one that corresponds to their actual losses and isn't more than 5% of the monthly rent—are unlikely to be successfully challenged in court by a tenant. (California)

[2] Landlords may not charge a late fee until nine days after rent is due. (Connecticut)

[3] To charge a late fee, landlord must maintain an office in the county where the rental unit is located at which tenants can pay rent. If a landlord doesn't have a local office for this purpose, tenant has three extra days (beyond the due date) to pay rent before the landlord can charge a late fee. Late fee cannot exceed 5% of rent and cannot be imposed until the rent is more than five days late. (Delaware)

[4] Late fees cannot exceed ten dollars per day or $40 per month. (Iowa)

[5] Late fees cannot exceed 4% of the amount due for 30 days. Landlord must notify tenants, in writing, of any late fee at the start of the tenancy, and cannot impose it until rent is 15 days late. (Maine)

[6] Late fees cannot exceed 5% of the rent due. (Maryland)

[7] Late fees, including interest on late rent, may not be imposed until the rent is 30 days late. (Massachusetts)

State	When Rent Is Due	Grace Period	Where Rent Is Due	Late Fees
State Rent Rules (continued)				
Michigan	*Hilsendegen v. Scheich,* 21 N.W. 2d 894 (1885)			
Minnesota				
Mississippi				
Missouri				
Montana	Mont. Code Ann. § 70-24-201(2)(c)		Mont. Code Ann. § 70-24-201(2)(b)	
Nebraska	Neb. Rev. Stat. § 76-1414(3)		Neb. Rev. Stat. § 76-1414(3)	
Nevada	Nev. Rev. Stat. Ann. §§ 118A.210			Nev. Rev. Stat. Ann. § 118A.200(2)(g), (3)(c)
New Hampshire				
New Jersey				N.J. Stat. Ann. § 2A:42-6.1 [8]
New Mexico	N.M. Stat. Ann. § 47-8-15(B)		N.M. Stat. Ann. § 47-8-15(B)	N.M. Stat. Ann § 47-8-15(D) [9]
New York				
North Carolina		N.C. Gen Stat. § 42-46		N.C. Gen. Stat. § 42-46 [10]
North Dakota	N.D. Cent. Code § 47-16-07			
Ohio				
Oklahoma	Okla. Stat. Ann. tit. 41, § 109		Okla. Stat. Ann. tit. 41, § 109	*Sun Ridge Investors, Ltd. v. Parker,* 956 P.2d 876 (1998) [11]
Oregon	Or. Rev. Stat. § 90.240(5)(a)	Or. Rev. Stat. § 90.260	Or. Rev. Stat. § 90.240(5)(a)	Or. Rev. Stat. § 90.260 [12]
Pennsylvania				
Rhode Island	R.I. Gen. Laws § 34-18-15(c)	R.I. Gen. Laws § 34-18-35	R.I. Gen. Laws § 34-18-15(c)	
South Carolina	S.C. Code Ann. § 27-40-310(c)		S.C. Code Ann. § 27-40-310(c)	
South Dakota	S.D. Codified Laws Ann. § 43-32-12			
Tennessee	Tenn. Code Ann. § 66-28-201(c)	Tenn. Code Ann. § 66-28-201(d)	Tenn. Code Ann. § 66-28-201(c)	Tenn. Code Ann. § 66-28-201(d) [13]
Texas				
Utah				
Vermont				
Virginia	Va. Code Ann. § 55-248.7(C)			
Washington				
West Virginia				
Wisconsin				
Wyoming				

[8] Landlord must wait until five days before charging a late fee. (New Jersey)

[9] Late fee may not exceed 10% of the rent specified per rental period. (New Mexico)

[10] Late fee cannot be higher than $15 or 5% of the rental payment, whichever is greater, and may not be imposed until the tenant is five days late paying rent. (North Carolina)

[11] Preset late fees are invalid. (Oklahoma)

[12] Landlord must wait four days after the rent due date to assess a late fee, and must disclose the late fee policy in the rental agreement. A flat fee must be "reasonable." A daily late fee may not be more than 6% of a reasonable flat fee, and cannot add up to more than 5% of the monthly fee.

[13] Landlord can't charge late fee until five days have passed. If day five is a Saturday, Sunday or legal holiday, landlord cannot impose a fee if the rent is paid on the next business day. Fee can't exceed 10% of the amount past due. (Tennessee)

State Security Deposit Rules

Here are citations for statutes pertaining to security deposits in each state. Details on various aspects of security deposits are provided in the chapters.

This table is limited to security deposit statutes. Some states—Alabama, Idaho and West Virginia—do not have statutes on security deposits. That doesn't mean that there is no law on the subject. Court decisions (what lawyers call "case law") in your state may set out quite specific requirements for refunding of deposits, whether they should be held in interest-bearing accounts and the like. This book does not cover all case or local law. To find out whether courts or local governments in your state have made decisions or ordinances you need to be aware of, you may need to do some legal research on your own.

State	Statute	Limit	Separate Account	Interest	Deadline for Landlord to Itemize and Return Deposit	Exemptions
Alabama	No statute	No statutory limit			No statutory deadline	
Alaska	Alaska Stat. § 34.03.070	Two months' rent, where rent exceeds $2,000 per month	✔		14 days if the tenant gives proper notice to terminate tenancy; 30 days if the tenant does not give proper notice	Any rental unit where the rent exceeds $2,000 per month
Arizona	Ariz. Rev. Stat. Ann. § 33-1321	One and one-half months' rent (unless tenant voluntarily agrees to pay more)			14 days	
Arkansas	Ark. Code Ann. §§ 16-303 to -306, 18-16-303 to 306	Two months' rent			30 days	Landlord who owns five or fewer rental units, unless these units are managed by a third party for a fee
California	Cal. Civ. Code §§ 1950.5, 1940.5(g)	Two months' rent (unfurnished, no waterbed); two and one-half months' rent (unfurnished, tenant has waterbed); three months' rent (furnished, no waterbed); three and one-half months' rent (furnished, tenant has waterbed)			Three weeks	
Colorado	Colo. Rev. Stat. §§ 38-12-102 to -104	No statutory limit			One month, unless lease agreement specifies longer period of time (which may be no more than 60 days); 72 hours (not counting weekends or holidays) if a hazardous condition involving gas equipment requires tenant to vacate	
Connecticut	Conn. Gen. Stat. Ann. § 47a-21	Two months' rent (tenant under 62 years of age); one month's rent (tenant 62 years of age or older)	✔	✔	30 days, or within 15 days of receiving tenant's forwarding address, whichever is later	
Delaware	Del. Code. Ann. tit. 25, § 5514	One month's rent on leases for one year or more; no limit for month-to-month rental agreements	✔		20 days	

State	Statute	Limit	Separate Account	Interest	Deadline for Landlord to Itemize and Return Deposit	Exemptions
District of Columbia	D.C. Code Ann § 42.3502.17 and D.C. Mun. Regs. tit. 14, §§ 308 to 311	One month's rent	✔	✔	45 days	
Florida	Fla. Stat. Ann §§ 83.49, 83.43 (11)	No statutory limit	✔	[1]	15 to 60 days depending on whether tenant disputes deductions	
Georgia	Ga. Code Ann. §§ 44-7-30 to 44-7-37	No statutory limit	✔		One month	Landlord who owns ten or fewer rental units, unless these units are managed by an outside party
Hawaii	Haw. Rev. Stat. § 521-44	One month's rent			14 days	
Idaho	Idaho Code § 6-321	No statutory limit			21 days or up to 30 days if landlord and tenant agree	
Illinois	765 Ill. Comp. Stat. 710/0.01 to 715/3	No statutory limit		✔ [2]	30 to 45 days depending on whether tenant disputes deductions	Landlord who owns four or fewer dwelling units
Indiana	Ind. Code Ann. §§ 32-31-31 to 32-31-3-19	No statutory limit			45 days	
Iowa	Iowa Code Ann. § 562A.12	Two months' rent	✔	[1]	30 days	
Kansas	Kan. Stat. Ann. § 58-2550	One month's rent (unfurnished, no pets); one and one-half months' rent (unfurnished with pets or furnished with no pets)			30 days	
Kentucky	Ky. Rev. Stat. Ann. § 383.580	No statutory limit	✔		30 to 60 days depending on whether tenant disputes deductions	
Louisiana	La. Rev. Stat. Ann. §§ 9:3251 to 3254	No statutory limit			One month	
Maine	Me. Rev. Stat. Ann. tit. 14, §§ 6031 to 6038	Two months' rent	✔		30 days (if written rental agreement) or 21 days (if tenancy at will)	Rental unit which is part of structure with five or fewer units, one of which is occupied by landlord
Maryland	Md. Code Ann. [Real Prop.] § 8-203 and § 8-203.1	Two months' rent	✔	✔	30 to 45 days depending on whether tenant has been evicted or has abandoned the premises	
Massachusetts	Mass. Gen. Laws Ann. ch. 186, § 15B	One month's rent	✔	✔	30 days	
Michigan	Mich. Comp. Laws §§ 554.602 to 613	One and one-half months' rent	✔		30 days	

[1] Interest payments are not required, but when they are made, certain rules apply.

[2] Applies only to landlords with 25 or more rental units.

			Separate		Deadline for Landlord to	
State	Statute	Limit	Account	Interest	Itemize and Return Deposit	Exemptions
Minnesota	Minn. Stat. Ann. §§ 504B.175 to 504B.178	No statutory limit		✔	Three weeks after tenant leaves and landlord receives forwarding address; five days if tenant must leave due to building condemnation	
Mississippi	Miss. Code Ann. § 89-8-21	No statutory limit			45 days	
Missouri	Mo. Ann. Stat. §535.300	Two month's rent			30 days	
Montana	Mont. Code Ann. §§ 70-25-101 to -206	No statutory limit			30 days 10 days if no deductions	
Nebraska	Neb. Rev. Stat. § 76-1416	One month's rent (no pets); one and one-quarter months' rent (pets)			14 days	
Nevada	Nev. Rev. Stat. Ann. §§ 118A.240 -.250	Three months' rent			30 days	
New Hampshire	N.H. Rev. Stat. Ann §§ 540-A:5 to :8; 540-B:10	One month's rent or $100, whichever is greater; when landlord and tenant share facilities, no statutory limit	✔	✔	30 days For shared facilities, if the deposit is more than 30 days' rent, landlord must provide written agreement acknowled-ging receipt and specifying when deposit will be returned. If no written agreement, 20 days after tenant vacates	Landlord who leases a single-family residence and owns no other rental property, or landlord who leases rental units in an owner-occupied building of five units or less (exemption does not apply to any individual unit in owner-occupied building that is occupied by a person 60 years of age or older)
New Jersey	N.J. Stat. Ann. §§ 46:8-19 to-26	One and one-half months' rent	✔	✔	30 days; 5 days in case of fire, flood, condemnation or evacuation	Owner-occupied building with two or fewer units where tenant fails to provide 30 days' written notice to landlord invoking provisions of act
New Mexico	N.M. Stat. Ann. §§ 47-8-18	One month's rent (for rental agreement less than one year); no limit for leases of one year or more		✔	30 days	
New York	N.Y. Gen. Oblig. Law §§ 7-103 to 7-108	No statutory limit for nonregulated units	✔	✔	Reasonable time	Landlord who rents out non-regulated units in buildings with five or fewer units need not pay interest
North Carolina	N.C. Gen. Stat. §§ 42-50 to -56	One and one-half months' rent for month-to-month rental agreements; two months' rent if term is longer than two months	✔		30 days	

State Security Deposit Rules (continued)

State	Statute	Limit	Separate Account	Interest	Deadline for Landlord to Itemize and Return Deposit	Exemptions
North Dakota	N.D. Cent. Code § 47-16-07.1	One month's rent (or $1,500 if tenant has a pet)	✔	✔	30 days	
Ohio	Ohio Rev. Code Ann. § 5321.16	No statutory limit		✔	30 days	
Oklahoma	Okla. Stat. Ann. tit. 41, § 115	No statutory limit	✔		30 days	
Oregon	Or. Rev. Stat. § 90.300	No statutory limit			31 days	
Pennsylvania	68 Pa. Cons. Stat. Ann. §§ 250.511a to 512	Two months' rent for first year of renting; one month's rent during second and subsequent years of renting	✔	✔	30 days	
Rhode Island	R.I. Gen. Laws § 34-18-19	One month's rent			20 days	
South Carolina	S.C. Code Ann. § 27-40-410	No statutory limit			30 days	
South Dakota	S.D. Codified Laws Ann. § 43.32-6.1 and § 43-32-24	One month's rent (higher deposit may be charged if special conditions pose a danger to maintenance of the premises)			Two weeks to return entire deposit or a portion, and supply reasons for withholding; 45 days for a written, itemized accounting, if tenant requests it	
Tennessee	Tenn. Code Ann. § 66-28-301	No statutory limit	✔		No statutory deadline	
Texas	Tex. Prop. Code Ann. §§ 92.101 to 92.109	No statutory limit			30 days	
Utah	Utah Code Ann. §§ 57-17-1 to -5	No statutory limit			30 days, or within 15 days of receiving tenant's forwarding address, whichever is later	
Vermont	Vt. Stat. Ann. tit. 9, § 4461	No statutory limit			14 days	
Virginia	Va. Code Ann. § 55-248.15:1	Two months' rent		✔	45 days	
Washington	Wash. Rev. Code Ann. §§ 59.18.260 to .285	No statutory limit	✔		14 days	
W. Virginia	No statute	No statutory limit			No statutory deadline	
Wisconsin	Wisc. Admin. Code § ATCP 134.06	No statutory limit			21 days	
Wyoming	Wyo. Stat. 1-21-1207 to -1208	No statutory limit			30 days, or within 15 days of receiving tenant's forwarding address, whichever is later; 60 days if there is damage	

States That Require Landlords to Maintain a Separate Account for Security Deposits	
Alaska	"Wherever practicable," deposit must be held in trust account or by escrow agent.
Connecticut	
Delaware	
District of Columbia	
Florida*	Instead of keeping separate account, landlord can post surety bond.
Georgia*	Instead of keeping separate account, landlord can post surety bond.
Iowa	
Kentucky*	
Maine	Deposit must be unavailable to landlord's creditors.
Maryland	Deposit must be held in Maryland banking or savings institution.
Massachusetts	Deposit must be held in Massachusetts and be unavailable to the landlord's creditors.
Michigan*	
New Hampshire	
New Jersey	
New York*	
North Carolina*	
North Dakota	
Oklahoma	
Pennsylvania	
Tennessee*	
Washington	

* Landlords must give tenants written information on where the security deposit is being held.

States That Require Landlords to Pay Interest on Deposits

Connecticut

Interest payments must be made annually and at termination of tenancy. The interest rate must be equal to the average rate paid on savings deposits by insured commercial banks, as published by the Federal Reserve Board Bulletin in November of the prior year, but not less than 1.5%.

Dist. of Columbia

Interest payments at the prevailing passbook rate must be made at termination of tenancy.

Florida

Interest payments (if any—account need not be interest-bearing) must be made annually and at termination of tenancy. However, no interest is due a tenant who wrongfully terminates the tenancy before the end of the rental term. If landlord is paying interest, details on interest rate and time of payment must be provided in lease or rental agreement.

Illinois

Landlords who rent 25 or more units in either a single building or a complex of buildings located on contiguous properties must pay interest on deposits held for more than six months. Interest must be paid annually and at termination of tenancy.

Iowa

Interest payment (if any—account need not be interest-bearing) must be made at termination of tenancy. Interest earned during first five years of tenancy belongs to landlord.

Maryland

Interest must be paid (at an annual rate of 4%) only on security deposits of $50 or more, at six-month intervals, not compounded.

Massachusetts

Landlord must pay tenant 5% interest per year or the amount received from the bank where the deposit has been held. Interest should be paid to the tenant yearly, and within 30 days of termination date. Interest will not accrue for the last month for which rent was paid in advance.

Minnesota

Landlord must pay 3% (simple, noncompounded) annual interest until 5/1/04. After that, 4% per year. Any interest amount less than $1 is excluded.

New Hampshire

A landlord who holds a security deposit for a year or longer must pay interest at a rate equal to the interest rate paid on regular savings accounts in the New Hampshire bank, savings and loan association or credit union where it is deposited. If a landlord mingles security deposits in a single account, the landlord must pay the actual interest earned proportionately to each tenant. Upon request, a landlord must give the tenant the name of any institution where the security deposit is held, the account number, the amount on deposit and the interest rate on the deposit, and must allow the tenant to examine his security deposit records. A tenant may request the interest accrued every three years, 30 days before that year's tenancy expires. The landlord must comply with the request within 15 days of the expiration of that year's tenancy.

New Jersey

Landlord must place the deposit in an insured money market account or other account where the fund matures in one year or less. Landlord must pay tenant interest on account, minus an amount not to exceed 1% per annum of the amount invested, or 12.5% of the aggregate interest, whichever is higher, less the amount of any service fee charged by the financial institution holding the deposit.

New Mexico

Landlord who receives more than one month's rent deposit on a year lease must pay the tenant, annually, interest equal to the passbook interest.

New York

Interest must be paid at the "prevailing rate" on deposits received from tenants who are rent controlled or rent stabilized or who rent units in buildings containing six or more units. The landlord may retain an administrative fee of 1% per year on the sum deposited.

States That Require Landlords to Pay Interest on Deposits (continued)

North Dakota	Landlord must pay interest if the period of occupancy is at least nine months. Money must be held in a federally insured interest-bearing savings or passbook account.
Ohio	Any security deposit in excess of $50 or one month's rent, whichever is greater, must bear interest on the excess at the rate of 5% per annum if the tenant stays for six months or more. Interest must be paid annually and upon termination of tenancy.
Pennsylvania	Tenant who occupies rental unit for two or more years is entitled to interest beginning with the 25th month of occupancy. Landlord must pay tenant interest (minus fee of 1%) at the end of the third and subsequent years of the tenancy.
Virginia	Landlord must accrue interest at an annual rate equal to 1% below the Federal Reserve Board discount rate as of January 1 of each year, on all money held as security. No interest is payable unless the landlord holds the deposit for over 13 months after the date of the rental agreement for continuous occupancy of the same unit. Interest begins accruing from the effective date of the rental agreement and must be paid only upon termination of tenancy.

Attachment to Florida Leases and Rental Agreements (Security Deposits)

Fla. Stat. Ann. § 83.49(3)(a). Upon the vacating of the premises for termination of the lease, if the landlord does not intend to impose a claim on the security deposit, the landlord shall have 15 days to return the security deposit together with interest if otherwise required, or the landlord shall have 30 days to give the tenant written notice by certified mail to the tenant's last known mailing address of his or her intention to impose a claim on the deposit and the reason for imposing the claim. The notice shall contain a statement in substantially the following form:

This is a notice of my intention to impose a claim for damages in the amount of $ _____ upon your security deposit, due to _____. It is sent to you as required by s. 83.49(3), Florida Statutes. You are hereby notified that you must object in writing to this deduction from your security deposit within 15 days from the time you receive this notice or I will be authorized to deduct my claim from your security deposit. Your objection must be sent to _____ (landlord's address).

If the landlord fails to give the required notice within the 30-day period, he forfeits his right to impose a claim upon the security deposit.

(b) Unless the tenant objects to the imposition of the landlord's claim of the amount thereof within 15 days after receipt of the landlord's notice of intention to impose a claim, the landlord may then deduct the amount of his claim and shall remit the balance of the deposit to the tenant within 30 days after the date of the notice of intention to impose a claim for damages.

(c) If either party institutes an action in a court of competent jurisdiction to adjudicate the party's right to the security deposit, the prevailing party is entitled to receive his or her court costs plus a reasonable fee for his or her attorney. The court shall advance the cause on the calendar.

(d) Compliance with this section by an individual or business entity authorized to conduct business in this state, including Florida-licensed real estate brokers and salespersons, shall constitute compliance with all other relevant Florida Statutes pertaining to security deposits held pursuant to a rental agreement or other landlord-tenant relationship. Enforcement personnel shall look solely to this section to determine compliance. This section prevails over any conflicting provisions in chapter 475 and in other sections of the Florida Statutes, and shall operate to permit licensed real estate brokers to disburse security deposits and deposit money without having to comply with the notice and setlement procedures contained in s. 475.25(1)(d).

State Laws on Landlord's Access to Rental Property

This is a synopsis of state laws that specify circumstances when a landlord may enter rental premises and the amount of notice required for such entry.

State	State Law Citation	Amount of Notice Required in Nonemergency Situations	To Deal With an Emergency	To Inspect the Premises	To Make Repairs, Alterations or Improvements	To Show Property to Prospective Tenants or Purchasers	During Tenant's Extended Absence
			Reasons Landlord May Enter				
Alabama	No statute						
Alaska	Alaska Stat. § 34.03.140	24 hours	✔	✔	✔	✔	✔
Arizona	Ariz. Rev. Stat. Ann. § 33-1343	Two days	✔	✔	✔	✔	
Arkansas	No statute						
California	Cal. Civ. Code § 1954	24 hours (48 hours for initial move-out inspection)	✔	✔	✔		
Colorado	No statute						
Connecticut	Conn. Gen. Stat. Ann. §§ 47a-16 to -16a	Reasonable notice	✔	✔	✔	✔	✔
Delaware	Del. Code Ann. tit. 25, §§ 5509, 5510	Two days	✔	✔	✔	✔	✔
District of Columbia	No statute						
Florida	Fla. Stat. Ann. § 83.53	12 hours	✔	✔	✔	✔	✔
Georgia	No statute						
Hawaii	Haw. Rev. Stat. §§ 521-53, 521-70(b)	Two days	✔	✔	✔	✔	✔
Idaho	No statute						
Illinois	No statute						
Indiana	No statute						
Iowa	Iowa Code Ann. §§ 562A.19, .28, .29	24 hours	✔	✔	✔	✔	✔
Kansas	Kan. Stat. Ann. §§ 58-2557, -2565	Reasonable notice	✔	✔	✔	✔	✔
Kentucky	Ky. Rev. Stat. Ann. § 383.615	Two days	✔	✔	✔	✔	✔
Louisiana	No statute						
Maine	Me. Rev. Stat. Ann. tit. 14, § 6025	24 hours	✔	✔	✔	✔	
Maryland	No statute						
Massachusetts	Mass. Gen. Laws Ann. ch. 186, § 15B(1)(a)		✔	✔	✔		
Michigan	No statute						
Minnesota	Minn. Stat. Ann. § 504B.211	Reasonable notice	✔	✔	✔	✔	

State Laws on Landlord's Access to Rental Property (continued)

State	State Law Citation	Amount of Notice Required in Nonemergency Situations	To Deal With an Emergency	To Inspect the Premises	To Make Reparis, Alterations or Improvements	To Show Property to Prospective Tenants or Purchasers	During Tenant's Extended Absence
Mississippi	No statute						
Missouri	No statute						
Montana	Mont. Code Ann. § 70-24-312	24 hours	✔	✔	✔	✔	✔
Nebraska	Neb. Rev. Stat. § 76-1423	One day	✔	✔	✔	✔	✔
Nevada	Nev. Rev. Stat. Ann. § 118A.330	24 hours	✔	✔	✔	✔	
New Hampshire	N.H. Rev. Stat. Ann. § 540-A:3	Notice which is adequate under the circumstances	✔ Tenant's prior consent is necessary.				
New Jersey	No statute						
New Mexico	N.M. Stat. Ann. § 47-8-24	24 hours	✔	✔	✔	✔	✔
New York	No statute						
North Carolina	No statute						
North Dakota	N.D. Cent. Code § 47-16-07.3	Reasonable notice	✔	✔	✔	✔	
Ohio	Ohio Rev. Code Ann. §§ 5321.04(A,8), 5321.05(B)	24 hours	✔	✔	✔	✔	
Oklahoma	Okla. Stat. Ann. tit. 41, § 128	One day	✔	✔	✔	✔	
Oregon	Or. Rev. Stat. § 90.322	24 hours	✔	✔	✔	✔	
Pennsylvania	No statute						
Rhode Island	R.I. Gen. Laws § 34-18-26	Two days	✔	✔	✔	✔	✔
South Carolina	S.C. Code Ann. § 27-40-530	24 hours	✔	✔	✔	✔	✔
South Dakota	No statute						
Tennessee	Tenn. Code Ann. § 66-28-403	✔	✔	✔	✔	✔	
Texas	No statute						
Utah	Utah Code Ann. § 57-22-5(2)(c)	✔	✔				
Vermont	Vt. Stat. Ann. tit. 9, § 4460	48 hours	✔	✔	✔	✔	
Virginia	Va. Code Ann. § 55-248.18	24 hours	✔	✔	✔	✔	✔
Washington	Wash. Rev. Code Ann. § 59.18.150	Two days	✔	✔	✔	✔	
West Virginia	No statute						
Wisconsin	Wis. Stat. Ann. § 704.05(2)	Reasonable notice	✔	✔	✔	✔	
Wyoming	No statute						

Tear-Out Forms

Month-to-Month Residential Rental Agreement

Clause 1. Identification of Landlord and Tenant

This Agreement is entered into between _____

_____ ("Tenant") and

_____ ("Landlord").

Each Tenant is jointly and severally liable for the payment of rent and performance of all other terms of this Agreement.

Clause 2. Identification of Premises

Subject to the terms and conditions in this Agreement, Landlord rents to Tenant, and Tenant rents from Landlord, for residential purposes only, the premises located at _____

_____ ("the premises"),

together with the following furnishings and appliances: _____

_____ .

Rental of the premises also includes _____

_____ .

Clause 3. Limits on Use and Occupancy

The premises are to be used only as a private residence for Tenant(s) listed in Clause 1 of this Agreement, and their minor children. Occupancy by guests for more than _____ is prohibited without Landlord's written consent and will be considered a breach of this Agreement.

Clause 4. Term of the Tenancy

The rental will begin on _____, 200____, and continue on a month-to-month basis. Landlord may terminate the tenancy or modify the terms of this Agreement by giving the Tenant _____ days' written notice. Tenant may terminate the tenancy by giving the Landlord _____ days' written notice.

Clause 5. Payment of Rent

Regular monthly rent.

Tenant will pay to Landlord a monthly rent of $_____ , payable in advance on the first day of each month, except when that day falls on a weekend or legal holiday, in which case rent is due on the next business day. Rent will be paid in the following manner unless Landlord designates otherwise:

Delivery of payment.

> Rent will be paid:

> ☐ by mail, to _____

> ☐ in person, at _____

Form of payment.

> Landlord will accept payment in these forms:

> ☐ personal check made payable to _____

> ☐ cashier's check made payable to _____

> ☐ credit card

> ☐ money order

> ☐ cash

Prorated first month's rent.

> For the period from Tenant's move-in date, _____, 200____, through

the end of the month, Tenant will pay to Landlord the prorated monthly rent of $_____.

This amount will be paid on or before the date the Tenant moves in.

Clause 6.   Late Charges

> If Tenant fails to pay the rent in full before the end of the _____ day after it's due, Tenant

will pay Landlord a late charge as follows:_____

_____.

Landlord does not waive the right to insist on payment of the rent in full on the date it is due.

Clause 7.   Returned Check and Other Bank Charges

> If any check offered by Tenant to Landlord in payment of rent or any other amount due under this

Agreement is returned for lack of sufficient funds, a "stop payment" or any other reason, Tenant will pay

Landlord a returned check charge of $_____.

Clause 8.   Security Deposit

> On signing this Agreement, Tenant will pay to Landlord the sum of $_____ as a security

deposit. Tenant may not, without Landlord's prior written consent, apply this security deposit to the last

month's rent or to any other sum due under this Agreement. Within _____

after Tenant has vacated the premises, returned keys and provided Landlord with a forwarding address,

Landlord will return the deposit in full or give Tenant an itemized written statement of the reasons for, and

the dollar amount of, any of the security deposit retained by Landlord, along with a check for any

deposit balance.

Clause 9. Utilities

Tenant will pay all utility charges, except for the following, which will be paid by Landlord:

_____

_____ .

Clause 10. Assignment and Subletting

Tenant will not sublet any part of the premises or assign this Agreement without the prior written consent of Landlord.

Clause 11. Tenant's Maintenance Responsibilities

Tenant will: (1) keep the premises clean, sanitary and in good condition and, upon termination of the tenancy, return the premises to Landlord in a condition identical to that which existed when Tenant took occupancy, except for ordinary wear and tear; (2) immediately notify Landlord of any defects or dangerous conditions in and about the premises of which Tenant becomes aware; and (3) reimburse Landlord, on demand by Landlord, for the cost of any repairs to the premises damaged by Tenant or Tenant's guests or business invitees through misuse or neglect.

Tenant has examined the premises, including appliances, fixtures, carpets, drapes and paint, and has found them to be in good, safe and clean condition and repair, except as noted in the Landlord/ Tenant Checklist.

Clause 12. Repairs and Alterations by Tenant

    a.   Except as provided by law, or as authorized by the prior written consent of Landlord, Tenant will not make any repairs or alterations to the premises, including nailing holes in the walls or painting the rental unit.

    b.   Tenant will not, without Landlord's prior written consent, alter, re-key or install any locks to the premises or install or alter any burglar alarm system. Tenant will provide Landlord with a key or keys capable of unlocking all such re-keyed or new locks as well as instructions on how to disarm any altered or new burglar alarm system.

Clause 13. Violating Laws and Causing Disturbances

    Tenant is entitled to quiet enjoyment of the premises. Tenant and guests or invitees will not use the premises or adjacent areas in such a way as to: (1) violate any law or ordinance, including laws prohibiting the use, possession or sale of illegal drugs; (2) commit waste (severe property damage); or (3) create a nuisance by annoying, disturbing, inconveniencing or interfering with the quiet enjoyment and peace and quiet of any other tenant or nearby resident.

Clause 14. Pets

    No animal, bird or other pet will be kept on the premises, even temporarily, except properly trained dogs needed by blind, deaf or disabled persons and _____

under the following conditions: _____

_____

_____ .

Clause 15. Landlord's Right to Access

    Landlord or Landlord's agents may enter the premises in the event of an emergency, to make repairs or improvements or to show the premises to prospective buyers or tenants. Landlord may also enter the premises to conduct an annual inspection to check for safety or maintenance problems. Except in cases of emergency, Tenant's abandonment of the premises, court order or where it is impractical to do so, Landlord shall give Tenant _____ notice before entering.

Clause 16. Extended Absences by Tenant

    Tenant will notify Landlord in advance if Tenant will be away from the premises for _____ or more consecutive days. During such absence, Landlord may enter the premises at times reasonably necessary to maintain the property and inspect for needed repairs.

Clause 17. Possession of the Premises

a. Tenant's failure to take possession.

If, after signing this Agreement, Tenant fails to take possession of the premises, Tenant will still be responsible for paying rent and complying with all other terms of this Agreement.

b. Landlord's failure to deliver possession.

If Landlord is unable to deliver possession of the premises to Tenant for any reason not within Landlord's control, including, but not limited to, partial or complete destruction of the premises, Tenant will have the right to terminate this Agreement upon proper notice as required by law. In such event, Landlord's liability to Tenant will be limited to the return of all sums previously paid by Tenant to Landlord.

Clause 18. Tenant Rules and Regulations

☐ Tenant acknowledges receipt of, and has read a copy of, tenant rules and regulations, which are attached to and incorporated into this Agreement by this reference.

Clause 19. Payment of Court Costs and Attorney Fees in a Lawsuit

In any action or legal proceeding to enforce any part of this Agreement, the prevailing party

☐ shall not / ☐ shall recover reasonable attorney fees and court costs.

Clause 20. Disclosures

Tenant acknowledges that Landlord has made the following disclosures regarding the premises:

☐ Disclosure of Information on Lead-Based Paint and/or Lead-Based Paint Hazards

☐ Other disclosures:

_____

_____

_____

Clause 21. Authority to Receive Legal Papers

The Landlord, any person managing the premises and anyone designated by the Landlord are authorized to accept service of process and receive other notices and demands, which may be delivered to:

☐ The Landlord, at the following address: _____

_____

☐ The manager, at the following address: _____

_____

☐ The following person, at the following address: _____

_____

Clause 22. Additional Provisions

Additional provisions are as follows: _____

_____

_____

_____

_____

_____

_____

_____

_____ .

Clause 23. Validity of Each Part

If any portion of this Agreement is held to be invalid, its invalidity will not affect the validity or enforceability of any other provision of this Agreement.

Clause 24. Grounds for Termination of Tenancy

The failure of Tenant or guests or invitees to comply with any term of this Agreement is grounds for termination of the tenancy, with appropriate notice to Tenant and procedures as required by law.

Clause 25. Entire Agreement

This document constitutes the entire Agreement between the parties, and no promises or representations, other than those contained here and those implied by law, have been made by Landlord or Tenant. Any modifications to this Agreement must be in writing signed by Landlord and Tenant.

_____ _____ _____
Date   Landlord or Landlord's Agent   Title

_____
Street Address

_____ _____
City, State & Zip   Phone

_____ _____ _____
Date   Tenant   Phone

_____ _____ _____
Date   Tenant   Phone

_____ _____ _____
Date   Tenant   Phone

Contrato Mensual De Arrendamiento

Cláusula 1. Identificación del Arrendador y de los Inquilinos.

Este Contrato es preparado y efectivo a partir de _____,

entre _____ ("Inquilinos")

y _____ ("Arrendador").

Cada Inquilino es conjunta y seriamente responsable del pago de renta y del cumplimiento de todos los

demás términos de este Contrato.

Cláusula 2. Identificación de la Propiedad.

De acuerdo con los términos y condiciones referidas en este Contrato, el Arrendador renta al

Inquilino, y éste renta del Arrendador, sólamente para residir, la propiedad ubicada en _____

_____ , ("la propiedad"),

junto con el mobiliario y los aparatos electrodomésticos siguientes: _____

_____

La renta de la propiedad también incluye _____

_____

Cláusula 3. Limitaciones en el Uso y Ocupación.

La propiedad se utilizará sólo como residencia privada por el Inquilino designado en la Cláusula 1

de este Contrato y sus hijos menores. Está prohibido que invitados habiten la propiedad por más de

_____, excepto con previo consentimiento por escrito del Arrendador. De lo contrario,

será considerado como una violación a este Contrato.

Cláusula 4. Período de Arrendamiento.

La renta comenzará el día _____ de _____ de _____, y podrá

continuarse el arrendamiento, mediante la renovación por cada mes. El Arrendador puede dar por

terminado este Contrato o modificar sus términos, siempre que notifique por escrito, al Inquilino, con

_____ días de anticipación. El Inquilino puede terminar este Contrato, notificándoselo al

Arrendador por escrito y con _____ días de anticipación.

Cláusula 5. Renta y Fechas de Pago.

Renta Regular Mensual.

El Inquilino pagará por adelantado, una renta mensual de $ _____ , el primer día del

mes; excepto cuando éste sea en un fin de semana o en un día feriado oficial, en cuyo caso deberá ser

pagada el próximo día laboral. Si no existe otra decisión por parte del Arrendador, la renta deberá ser

pagada de la manera siguiente:

Entrega de pago.

El arriendo será pagado:

☐ Por correo, dirigido a _____

☐ Personalmente, en _____

Forma de Pago.

El Arrendador recibirá los pagos en:

☐ Cheque Personal escrito en favor de _____

☐ Cheque de Caja escrito en favor de _____

☐ Tarjeta de Crédito

☐ Giro Postal

☐ Efectivo

Prorrateo del Primer mes de renta.

Para el período comenzando con la fecha en que se mudará el Inquilino, el día

_____ de _____ de _____ , hasta el fin del mes en curso,

el Inquilino pagará al arrendador la renta mensual prorrateada de $ _____. Esta suma se

pagará antes o en la fecha en que se mude el Inquilino a la propiedad.

Cláusula 6. Cobros por Mora.

Si el Inquilino falla en el pago total de la renta, antes del final del día siguiente a la fecha de pago,

tendrá que pagar costos por atrasos como se explica a continuación: _____

_____ .

El Arrendador no descartará el derecho de insistir en el pago total de la renta en la fecha debida.

Cláusula 7. Pagos por Cheques Sin Fondo y Recargos Bancarios.

En el caso de cualquier cheque, ofrecido por el Inquilino al Arrendador como pago de renta o

cualquier otra suma debida bajo este Contrato, sea regresado por insuficiencia de fondos, un "paro de

pago" o cualquier otra razón, el Inquilino deberá pagar un recargo por la cantidad de $_____.

Cláusula 8. Depósito de Garantía.

Al firmar el presente Contrato, el Inquilino pagará al Arrendador, la cantidad de $_____

como depósito de seguridad. Este depósito no puede aplicarse al último mes de renta o a cualquier

cantidad debida bajo este Contrato; excepto con previo consentimiento por escrito del Arrendador.

Dentro de _____ , después de que el Inquilino haya desocupado la

propiedad, haya entregado las llaves y proporcionado la dirección donde contactarse, el Arrendador le

entregará el depósito en su totalidad o le detallará de manera escrita, las razones y la cantidad que es

retenida por él, junto con un cheque por la cantidad de su diferencia.

Cláusula 9. Servicios Publicos.

El Inquilino pagará todos los servicios publicos, exceptuando los siguientes, los cuales serán

pagados por el Arrendador: _____

_____

Cláusula 10. Prohibición de Traspaso o Sub-arrendamiento.

El Inquilino no puede sub-arrendar cualquier parte de la propiedad o traspasar este Contrato, sin

previo consentimiento por escrito del Arrendador.

Cláusula 11. Responsabilidad del Inquilino de Mantenimiento de la propiedad.

El Inquilino acepta: (1) mantener la propiedad limpia e higiénica, en buena condición, y cuando el

arrendamiento termine, regresar la propiedad al Arrendador en idéntica condición a la que existía

cuando la habitaron, exceptuando el deterioro causado por el uso; (2) Notificar de inmediato al

Arrendador, sobre cualquier defecto o condición peligrosa que note en o alrededor de la propiedad; y

(3) reembolsar al Arrendador, bajo demanda de éste, los costos de cualquier reparación de daños a la

propiedad, ocasionados por uso indebido o negligencia del Inquilino o sus invitados.

El Inquilino ha revisado la propiedad, incluyendo los aparatos electro-domésticos, accesorios,

alfombras, cortinas y pintura, y los ha encontrado en buenas condiciones, seguras, y limpias,

exceptuando las que están en la Lista Arrendador-Inquilino.

Cláusula 12. Reparaciones y Modificaciones hechas por el Inquilino.

a. Exceptuando lo provisto por la ley o con la autorización previa y por escrito del Arrendador, el

Inquilino no debe hacer modificaciones o reparaciones en la propiedad, incluído el hacer hoyos en las

paredes o pintar el lugar.

b. El Inquilino no debe alterar las cerraduras, ni cambiarlas, ni instalar o modificar el sistema de alarma; excepto que haya recibido del Arrendador, una autorización previa y por escrito. El Inquilino deberá proveer al Arrendador una copia de llave o llaves para abrir cada cerradura modificada o nueva, así como instrucciones de cómo desarmar un sistema de alarma modificado o nuevo.

Cláusula 13. Causar Disturbios y Violaciones a la Ley.

El Inquilino tiene derecho al goce pacífico de la propiedad. Este y sus invitados no deben usar la propiedad o áreas aledañas, de manera que: (1) Viole cualquier ley o reglamento, incluyendo leyes que prohiben el uso, posesión o venta ilegal de drogas; (2) Permite el uso abusivo de la propiedad (daño serio a la propiedad); o (3) Cree un estorbo al molestar, provocar disturbios, provocar inconvenientes o interferir en el disfrute de paz y tranquilidad de otros inquilinos o vecinos.

Cláusula 14. Mascotas.

No se permite, ni siquiera temporalmente, tener ningún animal, pájaro u otros animales en la propiedad, excepto perros entrenados para auxiliar a ciegos, sordos o personas con incapacidades físicas, y _____

bajo las condiciones siguientes: _____

_____

_____.

Cláusula 15. Derecho del Arrendador al Acceso a la Propiedad.

El Arrendador o agentes de éste pueden entrar a la propiedad, en caso de emergencia, para hacer reparaciones o mejoras, o para mostrar la propiedad a potenciales nuevos inquilinos o compradores en perspectiva. También podrá entrar para la inspección anual para revisar la seguridad o chequear problemas de mantenimiento. Excepto en caso de emergencia, por el abandono de la propiedad por parte del Inquilino, orden de la corte, o cuando no sea práctico, el Arrendador deberá notificarle al Inquilino de su intención de entrar a la propiedad con _____ de anticipación.

Cláusula 16. Ausencias Prolongadas del Inquilino.

El Inquilino deberá previamente notificar al Arrendador, si estará ausente de la propiedad por _____ días consecutivos o más. Durante este tiempo, el Arrendador podrá entrar, cuando sea necesario, a la propiedad para inspeccionarla, para mantenimiento o para reparaciones necesarias.

Cláusula 17. Tomar Posesión de la propiedad.

a. Falla del Inquilino en tomar posesión de la propiedad.

Si después de haber firmado este Contrato, el Inquilino no toma posesión de la propiedad, aún será responsable por pago de la renta y cumplimiento de todos los demás términos de este Contrato.

b. Falla del Arrendador en entregar la propiedad.

Si el Arrendador no puede entregar la posesión de la propiedad al Inquilino, por cualquier razón fuera de su control, incluyendo, pero no limitado a, destrucción parcial o completa de la propiedad, el Inquilino tendrá el derecho de terminar este Contrato, mediante aviso previo y apropiado como lo señala la ley. En tal situación, la responsabilidad del Arrendador hacia el Inquilino, estará limitada a la devolución de todas las cantidades previamente pagadas por el Inquilino al Arrendador.

Cláusula 18. Normas y Regulaciones del Inquilino.

☐ El Inquilino reconoce lo recibido y que ha leído una copia de las Normas y Regulaciones del Inquilino; las cuales como referencia, están adjuntas e incorporadas al presente Contrato.

Cláusula 19. Pago del Abogado y Costos de la Corte en Caso de un Juicio.

En cualquier acción jurídico-legal para hacer cumplir total o parcialmente este Contrato, la parte prevaleciente

☐ No deberá / ☐ Deberá recuperar honorarios justos del abogado y costos de la corte.

Cláusula 20. Divulgaciones.

El Inquilino reconoce que el Arrendador le ha hecho las siguientes divulgaciones con respecto a la propiedad:

☐ Distribución de información sobre pintura a base de plomo y/o los peligros de este tipo de pintura.

☐ Otras divulgaciones:

_____

_____

_____.

Cláusula 21. Personal Autorizado para Recibir Documentos Legales.

El Arrendador, la persona que administre la propiedad, o a quien haya designado el Arrendador, están autorizados para aceptar servicio de proceso, y recibir otras noticias y demandas, las cuales pueden ser entregadas a:

☐ El Arrendador, a la siguiente dirección: _____

_____.

☐ El Administrador, a la siguiente dirección:_____

_____.

☐ A la persona designada, a la siguiente dirección:_____

_____.

Cláusula 22. Disposiciones Adicionales.

Disposiciones adicionales son las siguientes: _____

_____

_____

_____

_____

_____ .

Cláusula 23. Validez de las Cláusulas de este Contrato.

Si cualquier clausula de este Contrato es invalidado, ésto no afectará la validez o cumplimiento de las partes restantes de este Contrato.

Cláusula 24. Razones para Cancelar el Contrato de Arrendamiento.

El incumplimiento de cualesquiera de los términos de este Contrato, por parte del Inquilino o sus invitados, será razón para dar por cancelado el Contrato de arrendamiento, seguido con la debida notificación al Inquilino, de acuerdo con lo requerido por la ley.

Cláusula 25. Contrato Completo.

Este documento constituye el Contrato completo entre las partes, y el Arrendador y el Inquilino no han hecho otro compromiso, a no ser los contenidos en este Contrato o los señalados por la ley. Cualquier modificación al presente documento, debe ser por escrito y firmado por ambas partes.

_____ _____ _____

Fecha   Arrendador o su representante   Título

_____

Número y Nombre de la Calle

_____ _____ _____ _____

Ciudad   Estado   Código Postal   Teléfono

_____ _____ _____

Fecha   Nombre del Inquilino   Teléfono

_____ _____ _____

Fecha   Nombre del Inquilino   Teléfono

_____ _____ _____

Fecha   Nombre del Inquilino   Teléfono

Fixed-Term Residential Lease

Clause 1.   Identification of Landlord and Tenant

This Agreement is entered into between _____

_____ ("Tenant")

and _____ ("Landlord").

Each Tenant is jointly and severally liable for the payment of rent and performance of all other terms of this Agreement.

Clause 2.   Identification of Premises

Subject to the terms and conditions in this Agreement, Landlord rents to Tenant, and Tenant rents from Landlord, for residential purposes only, the premises located at _____

_____ ("the premises"),

together with the following furnishings and appliances: _____

_____.

Rental of the premises also includes _____

_____.

Clause 3.   Limits on Use and Occupancy

The premises are to be used only as a private residence for Tenant(s) listed in Clause 1 of this Agreement, and their minor children. Occupancy by guests for more than _____

is prohibited without Landlord's written consent and will be considered a breach of this Agreement.

Clause 4.   Term of the Tenancy

The term of the rental will begin on _____, 200____, and end on

_____, 200____. If Tenant vacates before the term ends, Tenant will be liable for the balance of the rent for the remainder of the term.

Clause 5.   Payment of Rent

Regular monthly rent.

Tenant will pay to Landlord a monthly rent of $_____ , payable in advance on the first day of each month, except when that day falls on a weekend or a legal holiday, in which case rent is due on the next business day. Rent will be paid in the following manner unless Landlord designates otherwise:

Delivery of payment.

Rent will be paid:

☐ by mail, to _____

☐ in person, at _____

Form of payment.

Landlord will accept payment in these forms:

☐ personal check made payable to _____

☐ cashier's check made payable to _____

☐ credit card

☐ money order

☐ cash

Prorated first month's rent.

For the period from Tenant's move-in date _____, 200____, through

the end of the month, Tenant will pay to Landlord the prorated monthly rent of $_____.

This amount will be paid on or before the date the Tenant moves in.

Clause 6.   Late Charges

If Tenant fails to pay the rent in full before the end of the _____ day after it's due, Tenant

will pay Landlord a late charge as follows: _____

_____.

Landlord does not waive the right to insist on payment of the rent in full on the date it is due.

Clause 7.   Returned Check and Other Bank Charges

If any check offered by Tenant to Landlord in payment of rent or any other amount due under this

Agreement is returned for lack of sufficient funds, a "stop payment" or any other reason, Tenant will pay

Landlord a returned check charge of $_____.

Clause 8.   Security Deposit

On signing this Agreement, Tenant will pay to Landlord the sum of $_____ as a security

deposit. Tenant may not, without Landlord's prior written consent, apply this security deposit to the last

month's rent or to any other sum due under this Agreement. Within _____

after Tenant has vacated the premises, returned keys and provided Landlord with a forwarding address,

Landlord will return the deposit in full or give Tenant an itemized written statement of the reasons for, and

the dollar amount of, any of the security deposit retained by Landlord, along with a check for any

deposit balance.

Clause 9. Utilities

Tenant will pay all utility charges, except for the following, which will be paid by Landlord:

_____

_____ .

Clause 10. Assignment and Subletting

Tenant will not sublet any part of the premises or assign this Agreement without the prior written consent of Landlord.

Clause 11. Tenant's Maintenance Responsibilities

Tenant will: (1) keep the premises clean, sanitary and in good condition and, upon termination of the tenancy, return the premises to Landlord in a condition identical to that which existed when Tenant took occupancy, except for ordinary wear and tear; (2) immediately notify Landlord of any defects or dangerous conditions in and about the premises of which Tenant becomes aware; and (3) reimburse Landlord, on demand by Landlord, for the cost of any repairs to the premises damaged by Tenant or Tenant's guests or business invitees through misuse or neglect.

Tenant has examined the premises, including appliances, fixtures, carpets, drapes and paint, and has found them to be in good, safe and clean condition and repair, except as noted in the Landlord/Tenant Checklist.

Clause 12. Repairs and Alterations by Tenant

a. Except as provided by law, or as authorized by the prior written consent of Landlord, Tenant will not make any repairs or alterations to the premises, including nailing holes in the walls or painting the rental unit.

b. Tenant will not, without Landlord's prior written consent, alter, re-key or install any locks to the premises or install or alter any burglar alarm system. Tenant will provide Landlord with a key or keys capable of unlocking all such re-keyed or new locks as well as instructions on how to disarm any altered or new burglar alarm system.

Clause 13. Violating Laws and Causing Disturbances

Tenant is entitled to quiet enjoyment of the premises. Tenant and guests or invitees will not use the premises or adjacent areas in such a way as to: (1) violate any law or ordinance, including laws prohibiting the use, possession or sale of illegal drugs; (2) commit waste (severe property damage); or (3) create a nuisance by annoying, disturbing, inconveniencing or interfering with the quiet enjoyment and peace and quiet of any other tenant or nearby resident.

Clause 14. Pets

No animal, bird or other pet will be kept on the premises, even temporarily, except properly trained dogs needed by blind, deaf or disabled persons and _____
under the following conditions: _____

_____

_____ .

Clause 15. Landlord's Right to Access

Landlord or Landlord's agents may enter the premises in the event of an emergency, to make repairs or improvements or to show the premises to prospective buyers or tenants. Landlord may also enter the premises to conduct an annual inspection to check for safety or maintenance problems. Except in cases of emergency, Tenant's abandonment of the premises, court order or where it is impractical to do so, Landlord shall give Tenant _____ notice before entering.

Clause 16. Extended Absences by Tenant

Tenant will notify Landlord in advance if Tenant will be away from the premises for _____ or more consecutive days. During such absence, Landlord may enter the premises at times reasonably necessary to maintain the property and inspect for needed repairs.

Clause 17. Possession of the Premises

a. Tenant's failure to take possession.

If, after signing this Agreement, Tenant fails to take possession of the premises, Tenant will still be responsible for paying rent and complying with all other terms of this Agreement.

b. Landlord's failure to deliver possession.

If Landlord is unable to deliver possession of the premises to Tenant for any reason not within Landlord's control, including, but not limited to, partial or complete destruction of the premises, Tenant will have the right to terminate this Agreement upon proper notice as required by law. In such event, Landlord's liability to Tenant will be limited to the return of all sums previously paid by Tenant to Landlord.

Clause 18. Tenant Rules and Regulations

☐ Tenant acknowledges receipt of, and has read a copy of, tenant rules and regulations, which are attached to and incorporated into this Agreement by this reference.

Clause 19. Payment of Court Costs and Attorney Fees in a Lawsuit

In any action or legal proceeding to enforce any part of this Agreement, the prevailing party ☐ shall not / ☐ shall recover reasonable attorney fees and court costs.

Clause 20. Disclosures

Tenant acknowledges that Landlord has made the following disclosures regarding the premises:

☐ Disclosure of Information on Lead-Based Paint and/or Lead-Based Paint Hazards

☐ Other disclosures:

_____

_____

_____

Clause 21. Authority to Receive Legal Papers

The Landlord, any person managing the premises and anyone designated by the Landlord are authorized to accept service of process and receive other notices and demands, which may be delivered to:

☐ The Landlord, at the following address: _____

_____

☐ The manager, at the following address: _____

_____

☐ The following person, at the following address: _____

_____

Clause 22. Additional Provisions

Additional provisions are as follows: _____

_____

_____

_____

_____

_____

_____ .

Clause 23. Validity of Each Part

If any portion of this Agreement is held to be invalid, its invalidity will not affect the validity or enforceability of any other provision of this Agreement.

Clause 24. Grounds for Termination of Tenancy

The failure of Tenant or Tenants's guests or invitees to comply with any term of this Agreement is grounds for termination of the tenancy, with appropriate notice to Tenant and procedures as required by law.

Clause 25. Entire Agreement

This document constitutes the entire Agreement between the parties, and no promises or representations, other than those contained here and those implied by law, have been made by Landlord or Tenant. Any modifications to this Agreement must be in writing signed by Landlord and Tenant.

_____   _____   _____
Date   Landlord or Landlord's Agent   Title

_____
Street Address

_____   _____
City, State & Zip   Phone

_____   _____   _____
Date   Tenant   Phone

_____   _____   _____
Date   Tenant   Phone

_____   _____   _____
Date   Tenant   Phone

Contrato De Arrendamiento Residencial A Plazo Fijo

Cláusula 1. Identificación del Arrendador y de los Inquilinos.

Este Contrato es preparado y efectivo a partir de _____,

entre _____ ("Inquilinos")

y _____ ("Arrendador").

Cada Inquilino es conjunta y seriamente responsable del pago de renta y del cumplimiento de todos los

demás términos de este Contrato.

Cláusula 2. Identificación de la Propiedad.

De acuerdo con los términos y condiciones referidas en este Contrato, el Arrendador renta al

Inquilino, y éste renta del Arrendador, sólamente para residir, la propiedad ubicada en _____

_____ , ("la propiedad"),

junto con el mobiliario y los aparatos electrodomésticos siguientes: _____

_____

La renta de la propiedad también incluye _____

_____

Cláusula 3. Limitaciones en el Uso y Ocupación.

La propiedad se utilizará sólo como residencia privada por el Inquilino designado en la Cláusula 1

de este Contrato y sus hijos menores. Está prohibido que invitados habiten la propiedad por más de

_____, excepto con previo consentimiento por escrito del Arrendador. De lo contrario,

será considerado como una violación a este Contrato.

Cláusula 4. Período de Arrendamiento.

La renta comenzará el día _____ de _____ de _____, y concluirá el día

_____ de _____ de _____. Si el Inquilino desocupa antes del vencimiento del

período de renta, será responsable por la diferencia de la renta que falta por el resto del término.

Cláusula 5. Renta y Fechas de Pago.

Renta Regular Mensual.

El Inquilino pagará por adelantado, una renta mensual de $ _____ , el primer día del

mes; excepto cuando éste sea en un fin de semana o en un día feriado oficial, en cuyo caso deberá ser

pagada el próximo día laboral. Si no existe otra decisión por parte del Arrendador, la renta deberá ser

pagada de la manera siguiente:

Entrega de pago.

El arriendo será pagado:

☐ Por correo, dirigido a _____

☐ Personalmente, en _____

Forma de Pago.

El Arrendador recibirá los pagos en:

☐ Cheque Personal escrito en favor de _____

☐ Cheque de Caja escrito en favor de _____

☐ Tarjeta de Crédito

☐ Giro Postal

☐ Efectivo

Prorrateo del Primer mes de renta.

Para el período comenzando con la fecha en que se mudará el Inquilino, el día

_____ de _____ de _____ , hasta el fin del mes en curso,

el Inquilino pagará al arrendador la renta mensual prorrateada de $ _____ . Esta suma se

pagará antes o en la fecha en que se mude el Inquilino a la propiedad.

Cláusula 6. Cobros por Mora.

Si el Inquilino falla en el pago total de la renta, antes del final del día siguiente a la fecha de pago,

tendrá que pagar costos por atrasos como se explica a continuación: _____

_____ .

El Arrendador no descartará el derecho de insistir en el pago total de la renta en la fecha debida.

Cláusula 7. Pagos por Cheques Sin Fondo y Recargos Bancarios.

En el caso de cualquier cheque, ofrecido por el Inquilino al Arrendador como pago de renta o

cualquier otra suma debida bajo este Contrato, sea regresado por insuficiencia de fondos, un "paro de

pago" o cualquier otra razón, el Inquilino deberá pagar un recargo por la cantidad de $_____ .

Cláusula 8. Depósito de Garantía.

Al firmar el presente Contrato, el Inquilino pagará al Arrendador, la cantidad de $_____

como depósito de seguridad. Este depósito no puede aplicarse al último mes de renta o a cualquier

cantidad debida bajo este Contrato; excepto con previo consentimiento por escrito del Arrendador.

Dentro de _____ , despúes de que el Inquilino haya desocupado la

propiedad, haya entregado las llaves y proporcionado la dirección donde contactarse, el Arrendador le

entregará el depósito en su totalidad o le detallará de manera escrita, las razones y la cantidad que es

retenida por él, junto con un cheque por la cantidad de su diferencia.

Cláusula 9. Servicios Publicos.

El Inquilino pagará todos los servicios publicos, exceptuando los siguientes, los cuales serán

pagados por el Arrendador: _____

_____

Cláusula 10. Prohibición de Traspaso o Sub-arrendamiento.

El Inquilino no puede sub-arrendar cualquier parte de la propiedad o traspasar este Contrato, sin

previo consentimiento por escrito del Arrendador.

Cláusula 11. Responsabilidad del Inquilino de Mantenimiento de la propiedad.

El Inquilino acepta: (1) mantener la propiedad limpia e higiénica, en buena condición, y cuando el

arrendamiento termine, regresar la propiedad al Arrendador en idéntica condición a la que existía

cuando la habitaron, exceptuando el deterioro causado por el uso; (2) Notificar de inmediato al

Arrendador, sobre cualquier defecto o condición peligrosa que note en o alrededor de la propiedad; y

(3) reembolsar al Arrendador, bajo demanda de éste, los costos de cualquier reparación de daños a la

propiedad, ocasionados por uso indebido o negligencia del Inquilino o sus invitados.

El Inquilino ha revisado la propiedad, incluyendo los aparatos electro-domésticos, accesorios,

alfombras, cortinas y pintura, y los ha encontrado en buenas condiciones, seguras, y limpias,

exceptuando las que están en la Lista Arrendador-Inquilino.

Cláusula 12. Reparaciones y Modificaciones hechas por el Inquilino.

a. Exceptuando lo provisto por la ley o con la autorización previa y por escrito del Arrendador, el

Inquilino no debe hacer modificaciones o reparaciones en la propiedad, incluído el hacer hoyos en las

paredes o pintar el lugar.

b. El Inquilino no debe alterar las cerraduras, ni cambiarlas, ni instalar o modificar el sistema de alarma; excepto que haya recibido del Arrendador, una autorización previa y por escrito. El Inquilino deberá proveer al Arrendador una copia de llave o llaves para abrir cada cerradura modificada o nueva, así como instrucciones de cómo desarmar un sistema de alarma modificado o nuevo.

Cláusula 13. Causar Disturbios y Violaciones a la Ley.

El Inquilino tiene derecho al goce pacífico de la propiedad. Este y sus invitados no deben usar la propiedad o áreas aledañas, de manera que: (1) Viole cualquier ley o reglamento, incluyendo leyes que prohiben el uso, posesión o venta ilegal de drogas; (2) Permite el uso abusivo de la propiedad (daño serio a la propiedad); o (3) Cree un estorbo al molestar, provocar disturbios, provocar inconvenientes o interferir en el disfrute de paz y tranquilidad de otros inquilinos o vecinos.

Cláusula 14. Mascotas.

No se permite, ni siquiera temporalmente, tener ningún animal, pájaro u otros animales en la propiedad, excepto perros entrenados para auxiliar a ciegos, sordos o personas con incapacidades físicas, y _____

bajo las condiciones siguientes: _____

_____

_____ .

Cláusula 15. Derecho del Arrendador al Acceso a la Propiedad.

El Arrendador o agentes de éste pueden entrar a la propiedad, en caso de emergencia, para hacer reparaciones o mejoras, o para mostrar la propiedad a potenciales nuevos inquilinos o compradores en perspectiva. También podrá entrar para la inspección anual para revisar la seguridad o chequear problemas de mantenimiento. Excepto en caso de emergencia, por el abandono de la propiedad por parte del Inquilino, orden de la corte, o cuando no sea práctico, el Arrendador deberá notificarle al Inquilino de su intención de entrar a la propiedad con _____ de anticipación.

Cláusula 16. Ausencias Prolongadas del Inquilino.

El Inquilino deberá previamente notificar al Arrendador, si estará ausente de la propiedad por _____ días consecutivos o más. Durante este tiempo, el Arrendador podrá entrar, cuando sea necesario, a la propiedad para inspeccionarla, para mantenimiento o para reparaciones necesarias.

Cláusula 17. Tomar Posesión de la propiedad.

a. Falla del Inquilino en tomar posesión de la propiedad.

Si después de haber firmado este Contrato, el Inquilino no toma posesión de la propiedad, aún será responsable por pago de la renta y cumplimiento de todos los demás términos de este Contrato.

b. Falla del Arrendador en entregar la propiedad.

Si el Arrendador no puede entregar la posesión de la propiedad al Inquilino, por cualquier razón fuera de su control, incluyendo, pero no limitado a, destrucción parcial o completa de la propiedad, el Inquilino tendrá el derecho de terminar este Contrato, mediante aviso previo y apropiado como lo señala la ley. En tal situación, la responsabilidad del Arrendador hacia el Inquilino, estará limitada a la devolución de todas las cantidades previamente pagadas por el Inquilino al Arrendador.

Cláusula 18. Normas y Regulaciones del Inquilino.

☐ El Inquilino reconoce lo recibido y que ha leído una copia de las Normas y Regulaciones del Inquilino; las cuales como referencia, están adjuntas e incorporadas al presente Contrato.

Cláusula 19. Pago del Abogado y Costos de la Corte en Caso de un Juicio.

En cualquier acción jurídico-legal para hacer cumplir total o parcialmente este Contrato, la parte prevaleciente

☐ No deberá / ☐ Deberá recuperar honorarios justos del abogado y costos de la corte.

Cláusula 20. Divulgaciones.

El Inquilino reconoce que el Arrendador le ha hecho las siguientes divulgaciones con respecto a la propiedad:

☐ Distribución de información sobre pintura a base de plomo y/o los peligros de este tipo de pintura.

☐ Otras divulgaciones:

_____

_____

_____

Cláusula 21. Personal Autorizado para Recibir Documentos Legales.

El Arrendador, la persona que administre la propiedad, o a quien haya designado el Arrendador, están autorizados para aceptar servicio de proceso, y recibir otras noticias y demandas, las cuales pueden ser entregadas a:

☐ El Arrendador, a la siguiente dirección: _____

_____

☐ El Administrador, a la siguiente dirección: _____

_____

☐ A la persona designada, a la siguiente dirección: _____

_____

Cláusula 22. Disposiciones Adicionales.

Disposiciones adicionales son las siguientes: _____

_____

_____

_____

_____

_____ .

Cláusula 23. Validez de las Cláusulas de este Contrato.

Si cualquier clausula de este Contrato es invalidado, ésto no afectará la validez o cumplimiento de las partes restantes de este Contrato.

Cláusula 24. Razones para Cancelar el Contrato de Arrendamiento.

El incumplimiento de cualesquiera de los términos de este Contrato, por parte del Inquilino o sus invitados, será razón para dar por cancelado el Contrato de arrendamiento, seguido con la debida notificación al Inquilino, de acuerdo con lo requerido por la ley.

Cláusula 25. Contrato Completo.

Este documento constituye el Contrato completo entre las partes, y el Arrendador y el Inquilino no han hecho otro compromiso, a no ser los contenidos en este Contrato o los señalados por la ley. Cualquier modificación al presente documento, debe ser por escrito y firmado por ambas partes.

_____   _____   _____

Fecha   Arrendador o su representante   Título

_____

Número y Nombre de la Calle

_____   _____   _____   _____

Ciudad   Estado   Código Postal   Teléfono

_____   _____   _____

Fecha   Nombre del Inquilino   Teléfono

_____   _____   _____

Fecha   Nombre del Inquilino   Teléfono

_____   _____   _____

Fecha   Nombre del Inquilino   Teléfono

Disclosure of Information on Lead-Based Paint or Lead-Based Paint Hazards

LEAD WARNING STATEMENT

Housing built before 1978 may contain lead-based paint. Lead from paint, paint chips and dust can pose health hazards if not managed properly. Lead exposure is especially harmful to young children and pregnant women. Before renting pre-1978 housing, lessors must disclose the presence of known lead-based paint and/or lead-based paint hazards in the dwelling. Lessees must also receive a federally approved pamphlet on lead poisoning prevention.

LESSOR'S DISCLOSURE

(a) Presence of lead-based paint and/or lead-based paint hazards. Check (i) or (ii) below:

☐ (i) Known lead-based paint and/or lead-based paint hazards are present in the housing (explain):_____.

☐ (ii) Lessor has no knowledge of lead-based paint and/or lead-based paint hazards in the housing.

(b) Records and reports available to the lessor. Check (i) or (ii) below:

☐ (i) Lessor has provided the lessee with all available records and reports pertaining to lead-based paint and/or lead-based paint hazards in the housing (list documents below):

_____

☐ (ii) Lessor has no reports or records pertaining to lead-based paint or lead-based paint hazards in the housing.

LESSEE'S ACKNOWLEDGMENT (INITIAL)

_____ (c) Lessee has received copies of all information listed above.

_____ (d) Lessee has received the pamphlet *Protect Your Family From Lead in Your Home.*

AGENT'S ACKNOWLEDGMENT (INITIAL)

_____ (e) Agent has informed the lessor of the lessor's obligations under 42 U.S.C. § 4852d and is aware of his/her responsibility to ensure compliance.

CERTIFICATION OF ACCURACY

The following parties have reviewed the information above and certify, to the best of their knowledge, that the information they have provided is true and accurate.

Lessor	Date	Lessor	Date
Lessee	Date	Lessee	Date
Agent	Date	Agent	Date

Declaración de Información sobre Pintura a Base de Plomo y/o Peligros de la Pintura a Base de Plomo

Declaración sobre los Peligros del Plomo

Se notifica a todo comprador de cualquier interés en propiedad real residencial en la cual fue construida una vivienda residencial antes del año 1978, que dicha propiedad puede presentar una exposición a plomo de la pintura a base de plomo que podría poner a niños jóvenes en situación de riesgo de desarrollar envenenamiento de plomo. El envenenamiento de plomo en niños jóvenes puede producir daños neurológicos permanentes, incluyendo incapacidad para el aprendizaje, cociente de inteligencia reducido, problemas de comportamiento y memoria dañada. El envenenamiento de plomo también representa un peligro especial para las mujeres embarazadas. El vendedor de cualquier interés en una propiedad privada real residencial tiene la obligación de proporcionarle al comprador toda la información que posea sobre los peligros de la pintura a base de plomo que se hayan determinado en evaluaciones o inspecciones de riesgo y de notificarle al comprador sobre cualquier peligro que conozca de la pintura a base de plomo. Se recomienda realizar una evaluación o inspección de posibles peligros de la pintura a base de plomo antes de la compra.

Declaración del Vendedor

(a) Presencia de pintura a base de plomo y/o peligros de pintura a base de plomo (marque (i) ó (ii) abajo):

    (i) _____ Confirmado que hay pintura a base de plomo y/o peligro de pintura a base de plomo en la vivienda (explique).

_____

    (ii) _____ El vendedor no tiene ningún conocimiento de que haya pintura a base de plomo y/o peligro de pintura a base de plomo en la vivienda.

(b) Archivos e informes disponibles para el vendedor (marque (i) ó (ii) abajo):

    (i) _____ El vendedor le ha proporcionado al comprador todos los archivos e informes disponibles relacionados con pintura a base de plomo y/o peligro de pintura a base de plomo en la vivienda (anote los documentos abajo).

_____

    (ii) _____ El vendedor no tiene archivos ni informes relacionados con pintura a base de plomo y/o peligro de pintura a base de plomo en la vivienda.

Acuse de Recibo del Comprador (inicial)

(c) _____ El comprador ha recibido copias de toda la información indicada arriba.

(d) _____ El comprador ha recibido el folleto titulado *Proteja a Su Familia del Plomo en Su Casa.*

(e) El comprador ha (marque (i) ó (ii) abajo):

    (i) _____ recibido una oportunidad por 10 días (o un período de tiempo de mutuo acuerdo) para hacer una evaluación o inspección de riesgo de presencia de pintura a base de plomo o de peligros de pintura a base de plomo; o

    (ii) _____ renunciado a la oportunidad de hacer una evaluación o inspección de riesgo de presencia de pintura a base de plomo o de peligros de pintura a base de plomo.

Acuse de Recibo del Agente (inicial)

(f) _____ El agente le ha informado al vendedor de las obligaciones del vendedor de acuerdo con 42 U.S.C. 4852(d) y está consciente de su responsabilidad de asegurar su cumplimiento.

Certificación de Exactitud

Las partes siguientes han revisado la información que aparece arriba y certifican que, según su entender, toda la información que han proporcionado es verdadera y exacta.

Vendedor	Fecha	Vendedor	Fecha
Comprador	Fecha	Comprador	Fecha
Agente	Fecha	Agente	Fecha

Are You Planning To Buy, Rent, or Renovate a Home Built Before 1978?

Many houses and apartments built before 1978 have paint that contains lead (called lead-based paint). Lead from paint, chips, and dust can pose serious health hazards if not taken care of properly.

By 1996, federal law will require that individuals receive certain information before renting, buying, or renovating pre-1978 housing:

LANDLORDS will have to disclose known information on lead-based paint hazards before leases take effect. Leases will include a federal form about lead-based paint.

SELLERS will have to disclose known information on lead-based paint hazards before selling a house. Sales contracts will include a federal form about lead-based paint in the building. Buyers will have up to 10 days to check for lead hazards.

RENOVATORS will have to give you this pamphlet before starting work.

IF YOU WANT MORE INFORMATION on these requirements, call the National Lead Information Clearinghouse at **1-800-424-LEAD**.

Protect Your Family From Lead in Your Home

EPA
United States
Environmental Protection
Agency

United States Consumer
Product Safety Commission

EPA747-K-94-001
May 1995

U.S. EPA Washington DC 20460
U.S. CPSC Washington DC 20207

Lead Gets in the Body in Many Ways

People can get lead in their body if they:

◆ Put their hands or other objects covered with lead dust in their mouths.

◆ Eat paint chips or soil that contains lead.

◆ Breathe in lead dust (especially during renovations that disturb painted surfaces).

Lead is even more dangerous to children than adults because:

◆ Babies and young children often put their hands and other objects in their mouths. These objects can have lead dust on them.

◆ Children's growing bodies absorb more lead.

◆ Children's brains and nervous systems are more sensitive to the damaging effects of lead.

1 out of every 11 children in the United States has dangerous levels of lead in the blood-stream.

Even children who appear healthy can have dangerous levels of lead.

IMPORTANT!

Lead From Paint, Dust, and Soil Can Be Dangerous If Not Managed Properly

FACT: Lead exposure can harm young children and babies even before they are born.

FACT: Even children that seem healthy can have high levels of lead in their bodies.

FACT: People can get lead in their bodies by breathing or swallowing lead dust, or by eating soil or paint chips with lead in them.

FACT: People have many options for reducing lead hazards. In most cases, lead-based paint that is in good condition is not a hazard.

FACT: Removing lead-based paint improperly can increase the danger to your family.

If you think your home might have lead hazards, read this pamphlet to learn some simple steps to protect your family.

Checking Your Family for Lead

A simple blood test can detect high levels of lead. Blood tests are important for:

◆ Children who are 6 months to 1 year old (6 months if you live in an older home with cracking or peeling paint).

◆ Family members that you think might have high levels of lead.

If your child is older than 1 year, talk to your doctor about whether your child needs testing.

Your doctor or health center can do blood tests. They are inexpensive and sometimes free. Your doctor will explain what the test results mean. *Treatment can range from changes in your diet to medication or a hospital stay.*

Get your children tested if you think your home has high levels of lead.

Where Lead-Based Paint Is Found

Many homes built before 1978 have lead-based paint. The federal government banned lead-based paint from housing in 1978. Some states stopped its use even earlier. Lead can be found:

◆ In homes in the city, country, or suburbs.

◆ In apartments, single-family homes, and both private and public housing.

◆ Inside *and* outside of the house.

◆ In soil around a home. (Soil can pick up lead from exterior paint, or other sources such as past use of leaded gas in cars.)

In general, the older your home, the more likely it has lead-based paint.

Lead's Effects

If not detected early, children with high levels of lead in their bodies can suffer from:

◆ Damage to the brain and nervous system

◆ Behavior and learning problems (such as hyperactivity)

◆ Slowed growth

◆ Hearing problems

◆ Headaches

Lead is also harmful to adults. Adults can suffer from:

◆ Difficulties during pregnancy

◆ Other reproductive problems (in both men and women)

◆ High blood pressure

◆ Digestive problems

◆ Nerve disorders

◆ Memory and concentration problems

◆ Muscle and joint pain

Brain or Nerve Damage

Hearing Problems

Slowed Growth

Digestive Problems

Reproductive Problems (Adults)

Lead affects the body in many ways.

Checking Your Home for Lead Hazards

You can get your home checked for lead hazards in one of two ways, or both:

◆ A paint inspection tells you the lead content of every painted surface in your home. It won't tell you whether the paint is a hazard or how you should deal with it.

◆ A risk assessment tells you if there are any sources of serious lead exposure (such as peeling paint and lead dust). It also tells you what actions to take to address these hazards.

Have qualified professionals do the work. *The federal government is writing standards for inspectors and risk assessors. Some states might already have standards in place.* Call your state agency for help with locating qualified professionals in your area (see page 12).

Trained professionals use a range of methods when checking your home, including:

◆ Visual inspection of paint condition and location.

◆ Lab tests of paint samples.

◆ Surface dust tests.

◆ A portable x-ray fluorescence machine.

Home test kits for lead are available, but recent studies suggest that they are not always accurate. Consumers should not rely on these tests before doing renovations or to assure safety.

Just knowing that a home has lead-based paint may not tell you if there is a hazard.

Where Lead Is Likely To Be a Hazard

Lead-based paint that is in good condition is usually not a hazard.

Peeling, chipping, chalking, or cracking lead-based paint is a hazard and needs immediate attention.

Lead-based paint may also be a hazard when found on surfaces that children can chew or that get a lot of wear-and-tear. These areas include:

◆ Windows and window sills.

◆ Doors and door frames.

◆ Stairs, railings, and banisters.

◆ Porches and fences.

Lead dust can form when lead-based paint is dry scraped, dry sanded, or heated. Dust also forms when painted surfaces bump or rub together. Lead chips and dust can get on surfaces and objects that people touch. Settled lead dust can reenter the air when people vacuum, sweep, or walk through it.

Lead in soil can be a hazard when children play in bare soil or when people bring soil into the house on their shoes. Call your state agency (see page 12) to find out about soil testing for lead.

Lead from paint chips, which you can see, and lead dust, which you can't always see, can both be serious hazards

What You Can Do Now To Protect Your Family

If you suspect that your house has lead hazards, you can take some immediate steps to reduce your family's risk:

◆ **If you rent, notify your landlord of peeling or chipping paint.**

◆ **Clean up paint chips immediately.**

◆ **Clean floors, window frames, window sills, and other surfaces weekly.** Use a mop or sponge with warm water and a general all-purpose cleaner or a cleaner made specifically for lead. REMEMBER: NEVER MIX AMMONIA AND BLEACH PRODUCTS TOGETHER SINCE THEY CAN FORM A DANGEROUS GAS.

◆ **Thoroughly rinse sponges and mop heads after cleaning dirty or dusty areas.**

◆ **Wash children's hands often, especially before they eat and before nap time and bed time.**

◆ **Keep play areas clean.** Wash bottles, pacifiers, toys, and stuffed animals regularly.

◆ **Keep children from chewing window sills or other painted surfaces.**

◆ **Clean or remove shoes before entering your home to avoid tracking in lead from soil.**

◆ **Make sure children eat nutritious, low-fat meals high in iron and calcium,** such as spinach and low-fat dairy products. Children with good diets absorb less lead.

How To Significantly Reduce Lead Hazards

In addition to day-to-day cleaning and good nutrition:

◆ You can **temporarily** reduce lead hazards by taking actions such as repairing damaged painted surfaces and planting grass to cover soil with high lead levels. These actions (called "interim controls") are not permanent solutions and will need ongoing attention.

◆ To **permanently** remove lead hazards, you must hire a lead "abatement" contractor. Abatement (or permanent hazard elimination) methods include removing, sealing, or enclosing lead-based paint with special materials. Just painting over the hazard with regular paint is not enough.

Removing lead improperly can increase the hazard to your family by spreading even more lead dust around the house.

Always use a professional who is trained to remove lead hazards safely.

Always hire a person with special training for correcting lead problems—someone who knows how to do this work safely and has the proper equipment to clean up thoroughly. If possible, hire a certified lead abatement contractor. Certified contractors will employ qualified workers and follow strict safety rules as set by their state or by the federal government.

Call your state agency (see page 12) for help with locating qualified contractors in your area and to see if financial assistance is available.

Other Sources of Lead

◆ **Drinking water.** Your home might have plumbing with lead or lead solder. Call your local health department or water supplier to find out about testing your water. You cannot see, smell, or taste lead, and boiling your water will not get rid of lead. If you think your plumbing might have lead in it:

- Use only cold water for drinking and cooking.

- Run water for 15 to 30 seconds before drinking it, especially if you have not used your water for a few hours.

While paint, dust, and soil are the most common lead hazards, other lead sources also exist.

◆ **The job.** If you work with lead, you could bring it home on your hands or clothes. Shower and change clothes before coming home. Launder your clothes separately from the rest of your family's.

◆ Old painted **toys** and **furniture.**

◆ Food and liquids stored in **lead crystal** or **lead-glazed pottery or porcelain.**

◆ **Lead smelters** or other industries that release lead into the air.

◆ **Hobbies** that use lead, such as making pottery or stained glass, or refinishing furniture.

◆ **Folk remedies** that contain lead, such as "greta" and "azarcon" used to treat an upset stomach.

Remodeling or Renovating a Home With Lead-Based Paint

Take precautions before you begin remodeling or renovations that disturb painted surfaces (such as scraping off paint or tearing out walls):

◆ **Have the area tested for lead-based paint.**

◆ **Do not use a dry scraper, belt-sander, propane torch, or heat gun** to remove lead-based paint. These actions create large amounts of lead dust and fumes. Lead dust can remain in your home long after the work is done.

If not conducted properly, certain types of renovations can release lead from paint and dust into the air.

◆ **Temporarily move your family** (especially children and pregnant women) out of the apartment or house until the work is done and the area is properly cleaned. If you can't move your family, at least completely seal off the work area.

◆ **Follow other safety measures to reduce lead hazards.** You can find out about other safety measures by calling 1-800-424-LEAD. Ask for the brochure "Reducing Lead Hazards When Remodeling Your Home." This brochure explains what to do before, during, and after renovations.

If you have already completed renovations or remodeling that could have released lead-based paint or dust, get your young children tested and follow the steps outlined on page 7 of this brochure.

State Health and Environmental Agencies

Some cities and states have their own rules for lead-based paint activities. Check with your state agency (listed below) to see if state or local laws apply to you. Most state agencies can also provide information on finding a lead abatement firm in your area, and on possible sources of financial aid for reducing lead hazards.

State/Region	Phone Number		
Alabama	(205) 242-5661	Missouri	(314) 526-4911
Alaska	(907) 465-5152	Montana	(406) 444-3671
Arkansas	(501) 661-2534	Nebraska	(402) 471-2451
Arizona	(602) 542-7307	Nevada	(702) 687-6615
California	(510) 450-2424	New Hampshire	(603) 271-4507
Colorado	(303) 692-3012	New Jersey	(609) 633-2043
Connecticut	(203) 566-5808	New Mexico	(505) 841-8024
Washington, DC	(202) 727-9850	New York	(800) 458-1158
Delaware	(302) 739-4735	North Carolina	(919) 715-3293
Florida	(904) 488-3385	North Dakota	(701) 328-5188
Georgia	(404) 657-6514	Ohio	(614) 466-1450
Hawaii	(808) 832-5860	Oklahoma	(405) 271-5220
Idaho	(208) 332-5544	Oregon	(503) 248-5240
Illinois	(800) 545-2200	Pennsylvania	(717) 782-2884
Indiana	(317) 382-6662	Rhode Island	(401) 277-3424
Iowa	(800) 972-2026	South Carolina	(803) 935-7945
Kansas	(913) 296-0189	South Dakota	(605) 773-3153
Kentucky	(502) 564-2154	Tennessee	(615) 741-5683
Louisiana	(504) 765-0219	Texas	(512) 834-6600
Massachusetts	(800) 532-9571	Utah	(801) 536-4000
Maryland	(410) 631-3859	Vermont	(802) 863-7231
Maine	(207) 287-4311	Virginia	(800) 523-4019
Michigan	(517) 335-8885	Washington	(206) 753-2556
Minnesota	(612) 627-5498	West Virginia	(304) 558-2981
Mississippi	(601) 960-7463	Wisconsin	(608) 266-5885
		Wyoming	(307) 777-7391

For More Information

The National Lead Information Center

Call **1-800-LEAD-FYI** to learn how to protect children from lead poisoning. For other information on lead hazards, call the center's clearinghouse at **1-800-424-LEAD**. For the hearing impaired, call, TDD **1-800-526-5456** (FAX: **202-659-1192,** Internet: **EHC@CAIS.COM**).

EPAõs Safe Drinking Water Hotline

Call **1-800-426-4791** for information about lead in drinking water.

Consumer Product Safety Commission Hotline

To request information on lead in consumer products, or to report an unsafe consumer product or a product-related injury call **1-800-638-2772.** (Internet: info@cpsc.gov). For the hearing impaired, call **TDD 1-800-638-8270.**

Local Sources of Information

Simple Steps To Protect Your Family From Lead Hazards

If you think your home has high levels of lead:

◆ Get your young children tested for lead, even if they seem healthy.

◆ Wash children's hands, bottles, pacifiers, and toys often.

◆ Make sure children eat healthy, low-fat foods.

◆ Get your home checked for lead hazards.

◆ Regularly clean floors, window sills, and other surfaces.

◆ Wipe soil off shoes before entering house.

◆ Talk to your landlord about fixing surfaces with peeling or chipping paint.

◆ Take precautions to avoid exposure to lead dust when remodeling or renovating (call 1-800-424-LEAD for guidelines).

◆ Don't use a belt-sander, propane torch, dry scraper, or dry sandpaper on painted surfaces that may contain lead.

◆ Don't try to remove lead-based paint yourself.

EPA Regional Offices

Your Regional EPA Office can provide further information regarding regulations and lead protection programs.

EPA Regional Offices

Region 1 (Connecticut, Massachusetts, Maine, New Hampshire, Rhode Island, Vermont)
John F. Kennedy Federal Building
One Congress Street
Boston, MA 02203
(617) 565-3420

Region 2 (New Jersey, New York, Puerto Rico, Virgin Islands)
Building 5
2890 Woodbridge Avenue
Edison, NJ 08837-3679
(908) 321-6671

Region 3 (Delaware, Washington DC, Maryland, Pennsylvania, Virginia, West Virginia)
841 Chestnut Building
Philadelphia, PA 19107
(215) 597-9800

Region 4 (Alabama, Florida, Georgia, Kentucky, Mississippi, North Carolina, South Carolina, Tennessee)
345 Courtland Street, NE
Atlanta, GA 30365
(404) 347-4727

Region 5 (Illinois, Indiana, Michigan, Minnesota, Ohio, Wisconsin)
77 West Jackson Boulevard
Chicago, IL 60604-3590
(312) 886-6003

Region 6 (Arkansas, Louisiana, New Mexico, Oklahoma, Texas)
First Interstate Bank Tower
1445 Ross Avenue, 12th Floor, Suite 1200
Dallas, TX 75202-2733
(214) 665-7244

Region 7 (Iowa, Kansas, Missouri, Nebraska)
726 Minnesota Avenue
Kansas City, KS 66101
(913) 551-7020

Region 8 (Colorado, Montana, North Dakota, South Dakota, Utah, Wyoming)
999 18th Street, Suite 500
Denver, CO 80202-2405
(303) 293-1603

Region 9 (Arizona, California, Hawaii, Nevada)
75 Hawthorne Street
San Francisco, CA 94105
(415) 744-1124

Region 10 (Idaho, Oregon, Washington, Alaska)
1200 Sixth Avenue
Seattle, WA 98101
(206) 553-1200

CPSC Regional Offices

Eastern Regional Center
6 World Trade Center
Vesey Street, Room 350
New York, NY 10048
(212) 466-1612

Central Regional Center
230 South Dearborn Street
Room 2944
Chicago, IL 60604-1601
(312) 353-8260

Western Regional Center
600 Harrison Street, Room 245
San Francisco, CA 94107
(415) 744-2966

¿Est Usted Planeando Comprar, Alquilar o Renovar una Casa Construida Antes de 1978?

Muchas casas y apartamentos construidos antes de 1978 tienen pintura que contiene plomo (llamada pintura a base de plomo). El plomo de la pintura, de los pedazos y del polvo pueden representar peligros serios para la salud si no se manejan con cuidado.

Para el año 1996 la ley federal requerir que las personas reciban cierta informacion antes de alquilar, comprar o renovar casas construidas antes de 1978:

Los **propietarios** tendrán que revelar la información que tienen a sus inquilinos sobre los peligros de la pintura a base de plomo antes que los contratos de arrendamiento (alquiler) entren en vigor.

Los **vendedores** de sus propiedades tendrn que revelar la información que tienen sobre los peligros de la pintura a base de plomo antes de vender una casa. Los contratos de venta incluirn un formulario federal sobre la pintura a base de plomo en el edificio. Los compradores tendrán hasta 10 días para verificar si hay peligros de plomo.

Los **renovadores** tendrn que entregarle a usted este folleto antes de comenzar un trabajo.

Si usted quiere obtener ms información sobre estos requisitos, llame al Centro de Información Nacional para Plomo (National Lead Information Clearinghouse) al **1-800-424-5323.**

Proteja a Su Familia del Plomo en Su Casa

EPA
Agencia de Protección Ambiental de los Estados Unidos (EPA)

Comisión de Seguridad de Productos de Consumo de los Estados Unidos

EPA747-K-94-001
Agosto 1995

U.S. EPA/CPSC Washington DC 20460
U.S. CPSC Washington DC 20207

El Plomo Entra en el Cuerpo de Muchas Maneras

El plomo puede entrar en los cuerpos de las personas si:

◆ Se meten las manos u otros objetos cubiertos de polvo de plomo en la boca.

◆ Comen pedazos de pintura o tierra que contiene plomo.

◆ Aspiran polvo de plomo (especialmente durante renovaciones de superficies pintadas).

El plomo es aún más peligroso para los niños que para los adultos porque:

◆ Los bebés y los niños pequeños con frecuencia se meten las manos y otros objetos en la boca. Estos objetos pueden tener polvo de plomo.

◆ Los cuerpos de los niños crecen y absorben más plomo que los de los adultos.

◆ Los sistemas nerviosos y los cerebros de los niños son más sensibles a los efectos dañinos del plomo.

1 de cada 11 niños en los Estados Unidos tiene niveles peligrosos de plomo en su cuerpo.

¡IMPORTANTE!

El Plomo de la Pintura, el Polvo y la Tierra Pueden Ser Peligrosos Si No Se Manejan Debidamente

Aviso: Exponer a los niños o bebes al plomo los puede dañar, incluso antes de nacer.

Aviso: Hasta los niños que parecen ser saludables pueden tener niveles peligrosos de plomo en sus cuerpos.

Aviso: El plomo puede entrar en los cuerpos de las personas cuando aspiran o tragan polvo de plomo, o si comen tierra o pedazos de pintura que contienen plomo.

Aviso: Las personas tienen muchas alternativas para reducir el peligro del plomo. En muchos casos, la pintura a base de plomo que est en buenas condiciones no es un peligro.

Aviso: Quitar la pintura a base de plomo incorrectamente puede aumentar el peligro para su familia.

Si usted piensa que su casa puede tener pintura a base de plomo, lea este folleto para conocer unas medidas sencillas que puede tomar para proteger a su familia.

Los Efectos del Plomo

Hasta los niños que parecen ser saludables pueden tener niveles peligrosos de plomo.

Si no se detecta temprano, los niños que tienen alto niveles de plomo en sus cuerpos pueden sufrir de:

◆ Daños al cerebro y al sistema nervioso

◆ Problemas de comportamiento y aprendizaje (tal como hiperactividad)

◆ Crecimiento lento

◆ Problemas para oír

◆ Dolores de cabeza

El plomo también es dañino para los adultos. Los adultos pueden sufrir de:

◆ Daño al bebé durante el embarazo

◆ Otros problemas reproductivos (en hombres y mujeres)

◆ Presión alta

◆ Problemas digestivos

◆ Trastornos nerviosos

◆ Problemas de memoria y de concentración

◆ Dolores musculares y de las articulaciones

Daños al Cerebro o a los Nervios

Problemas Para Oír

Crecimiento Retardado

Problemas Digestivos

Problemas de Reproducción (Adultos)

Examine a su Familia para Detectar el Plomo

Los exámenes de sangre son importantes para:

Un examen sencillo de la sangre puede detectar altos niveles de plomo.

◆ Niños que tienen entre 6 meses y 1 año (6 meses si usted vive en una casa o edificio que se está deteriorando, que puede tener plomo en la pintura).

◆ Miembros de la familia que usted cree que pueden tener altos niveles de plomo.

◆ Si su niño(a) tiene **más de 1 año,** hable con su médico sobre si su niño(a) necesita un examen.

Su médico o centro de salud pueden hacer los exámenes de la sangre. No son caros y a veces se hacen gratis. Su médico le explicará lo que significa el resultado de un examen. El tratamiento puede variar, desde cambios en el ambiente donde vive una persona y de sus hábitos de comer, hasta medicinas o una estencia en un hospital.

Dónde se Encuentra la Pintura a Base de Plomo

Muchas casas construidas antes de 1978 tienen pintura a base de plomo. En 1978, el Gobierno Federal prohibió la pintura a base de plomo para viviendas. Algunos estados ya habían prohibido su uso anteriormente. Se puede encontrar el plomo:

En general, mientras más antigua sea su casa, mayor será la probabilidad de que tenga pintura a base de plomo.

◆ En casas en la ciudad, en el medio rural o en los suburbios.

◆ En apartamentos, casas para una sola familia y en viviendas privadas y públicas.

◆ Adentro y afuera de la casa.

◆ En la tierra alrededor de la casa. (La tierra puede absorber el plomo de la pintura exterior o de otras fuentes como del uso en el pasado de gasolina con plomo en los autos.)

Cómo Verificar si su Casa Tiene Peligros de Plomo

Con sólo saber que una casa tiene pintura a base de plomo no le indica si hay peligro.

Usted puede verificar si su casa tiene plomo en una de dos maneras, o ambas:

◆ Una **inspección** de la pintura le indica el contenido de plomo de todas las superficies pintadas en su casa. No le indicará si la pintura es un peligro ni cómo usted la debería manejar.

◆ Una **evaluación del riesgo** le indica si hay fuentes de exposición seria al plomo (tales como pintura que se está pelando y polvo de plomo). Además, le indica qué acciones pueden ser tomadas para dirigirse a estos peligros.

Haga que inspectores calificados realicen las pruebas. El Gobierno Federal está preparando procedimientos y calificaciones universales para inspectores y evaluadores de riesgo que hacen pruebas de plomo. Posiblemente algunos estados ya tienen estándares vigentes. Llame a su agencia estatal para obtener más información sobre cómo encontrar a profesionales calificados en su área (vea la página 12).

Los profesionales entrenados usan una variedad de métodos cuando llevan a cabo sus pruebas, incluyendo:

◆ Inspección visual del lugar y la condición de la pintura.

◆ Examen de laboratorio de muestras de pintura.

◆ Pruebas del polvo de la superficie.

◆ Una máquina portátil de rayos-x de fluorescencia.

Hay paquetes de pruebas de plomo para la casa disponibles, pero estudios recientes indican que no siempre son confiables. Los consumidores no deben confiar en estas pruebas antes de hacer revonaciones o para asegurar que no hay peligro.

Dónde el Plomo Probablemente es un Peligro

La pintura a base de plomo que se está en buenas condiciones normalmente no es un peligro.

La pintura a base de plomo que se está pelando, despedazando o quebrando es un peligro y requiere atención inmediata.

La pintura a base de plomo también puede ser un peligro cuando se encuentra en superficies que los niños pueden morder o que tienen mucho uso.

La pintura a base de plomo es más peligrosa cuando está en la forma de pedazos de pintura, que usted puede ver, o de polvo de plomo, que usted no siempre puede ver.

◆ Ventanas y marcos de las ventanas.

◆ Puertas y marcos de las puertas.

◆ Escaleras, barandas y pasamanos.

◆ Portales, terrazas y cercas.

El polvo de plomo se puede formar cuando se raspa o lija en seco o se calienta la pintura a base de plomo. El polvo también se forma cuando las superficies pintadas (como puertas y ventanas) chocan o se juntan. Pedazos de plomo y polvo quedan en superficies que las personas tocan. El polvo de plomo que se acumula puede entrar en el aire cuando se usa una aspiradora o se barre.

El plomo en la tierra puede ser un peligro cuando los niños juegan allí o cuando las personas llevan tierra a la casa en los zapatos. Llame a su agencia estatal (en la lista en la parte de atrás de este folleto) para averiguar sobre pruebas de plomo para la tierra.

Qué Puede Hacer Usted Ahora Para Proteger a su Familia

Si usted sospecha que su casa tiene peligro de plomo, usted puede tomar algunas acciones inmediatamente para reducir el riesgo para su familia:

◆ Notifique a su propietario sobre pintura que se esté pelando o quebrando.

◆ Limpie los pedazos de pintura inmediatamente.

◆ Limpie los pisos, molduras y marcos de las ventanas y otras superficies semanalmente. Use un trapeador o una esponja con agua tibia y un detergente corriente o uno especial para plomo. **RECUERDE: Nunca mezcle productos de limpieza de amoníaco y de cloro, porque se produce un gas peligroso.**

◆ Enjuague completamente las esponjas y la cabeza de los trapeadores después de limpiar areas sucias o que tienen polvo. Bote los trapos que fueron usadós para limpiar.

◆ **Lávele las manos a los niños frecuentemente, especialmente antes de comer y antes de dormir la siesta y por la noche.**

◆ **Mantenga limpias las áreas de juego.** Limpie las botellas, chupetes, y juguetes periódicamente.

◆ **No deje que los niños muerdan las molduras de las ventanas u otras superficies pintadas.**

◆ Limpie o quítese los zapatos antes de entrar en su casa para que no entre el plomo de la tierra.

◆ **Asegúrese que los niños coman comidas nutritivas, bajas en grasa y con alto contenido de hierro y calcio,** tales como espinaca y productos lácteos bajos en grasa. Los niños que tienen buenas dietas absorben menos plomo.

Cómo Reducir los Peligros del Plomo Significativamente

Quitar el plomo indebidamente puede empeorar el peligro para su familia al regarse aen ms polvo de plomo por toda su casa.

Siempre consulte a un profesional que esté entrenado para hacer el trabajo debidamente y sin peligro.

Además de la limpieza diaria y la buena nutrición, usted puede considerar otras opciones para reducir los peligros del plomo.

◆ Usted puede reducir **temporalmente** los peligros del plomo tomando acciones como reparar superficies pintadas que han sido dañadas (vea la página siguiente) y sembrando grama o hierba para cubrir la tierra que tiene alto contenido de plomo. Estas acciones (llamadas "controles interinos") no son soluciones permanentes y no eliminarn todos los riesgos de exposición.

◆ Para quitar los peligros **permanentemente,** usted necesitará contratar a un especialista de "supresión". Los métodos de supresi n (o eliminación permanente de peligro) incluyen quitar, sellar o envolver la pintura a base de plomo con materiales especiales. **Simplemente pintar sobre el peligro con pintura corriente no es suficiente.**

Siempre contrate a una persona que tenga entrenamiento especial para corregir los problemas de plomo, alguien que sepa cómo hacer este trabajo sin peligro y que tenga el equipo necesario para limpiar debidamente después del trabajo. Si fuera posible, contrate a un especialista certificado para la supresión de plomo. Los especialistas **certificados** emplean a trabajadores calificados y cumplen las reglas estrictas de seguridad establecidas por el estado o por el Gobierno Federal.

Llame a su agencia estatal (vea la página 12) para que le ayuden a encontrar especialistas calificados en su área y para ver si hay ayuda financiera disponible.

Cómo Remodelar o Renovar una Casa que Tiene Pintura a Base de Plomo

Tome las precauciones antes de comenzar remodelaciones o renovaciones que puedan mover superficies pintadas (tales como ras-par la pintura o quitar paredes):

◆ **Examine el área para ver si hay pintura a base de plomo.**

◆ No use un raspador o una lijadora en seco, soplete de propano o pistola de alta temperatura para quitar la pintura a base de plomo. Estas acciones crean canti-dades grandes de polvo de plomo y gases. El polvo de plomo puede quedar en su casa un tiempo largo después que se ha terminado el trabajo.

Si no se hacen debidamente, ciertos tipos de renovaciones pueden soltar al aire el plomo de la pintura y polvo.

◆ **Mude temporalmente a su familia** (espe-cialmente a los niños y las mujeres embarazadas) fuera de la casa o del apartamento hasta que se haya termina-do el trabajo y limpiado debidamente el área. Si usted no puede mudar a su famil-ia, entonces por lo menos aisle completa-mente el rea de trabajo.

◆ **Tome otras medidas de seguridad para reducir los peligros del plomo.** Usted puede averiguar sobre otras medidas de seguridad llamando al 1-800-424-5323. Pida el folleto "Cómo Reducir los Peligros del Plomo al Remodelar Su Casa". Este folleto explica qué hacer antes, durante y después de renovaciones para evitar crear peligros basados en el plomo de larga duración.

Si usted ya ha completado renovaciones o remodelaciones que pueden haber soltado pintura o polvo a base de plomo, lleve a sus niños para que les hagan pruebas y siga los pasos indicados en la página 7 de este folleto.

Otras Fuentes de Plomo

◆ **Agua de beber.** Su casa puede tener tuberías de plomo o soldaduras de plomo. Llame a su departamento de salud local o abastecedor de agua para averiguar sobre cómo hacerle pruebas a su agua. Usted no puede ver, oler ni saborear el plomo, y hervir el agua no le quitará el plomo. Si usted cree que la plomería de su casa puede tener plomo:

 • **Use solamente agua fría para beber o cocinar.**

 • Deje correr el agua unos minutos antes de beberla, especialmente si usted no ha usado el agua por varias horas.

◆ **En el trabajo.** Si usted trabaja con plomo en su trabajo, usted podría llevar el plomo a su casa en sus manos o en su ropa. Dése una ducha y cámbiese la ropa antes de llegar a su casa. Lave la ropa suya separada a la de su familia.

◆ **Juguetes y muebles viejos pintados.**

◆ Alimentos y líquidos guardados en **cristalería a base de plomo o locería o porcelana con barniz a base de plomo.**

◆ Fábricas de fundición que trabajan con plomo u otras industrias que sueltan plomo en el aire.

◆ **Pasatiempos** que usan plomo, tales como alfarería o vidrios de color, o renovación de muebles.

◆ **Remedios caseros** que contienen plomo, tales como "greta" y "azarcón", que se usan para tratar la descomposición de estómago.

Agencias Estatales de Salud y de Protección Ambiental

Algunas ciudades y estados tienen sus propias regulaciones para las actividades relacionadas con pintura a base de plomo. Verifique con su agencia estatal (vea la lista abajo) para ver si hay leyes estatales o locales que le aplican a usted. Las agencias estatales también pueden proporcionar información sobre cómo encontrar una compañía de supresión de plomo en su área, y sobre posibles fuentes de asistencia financiera para reducir los peligros del plomo.

Estado/Región	Número de Teléfono	Estado/Región	Número de Teléfono
Alabama	(205) 242-5661	Montana	(406) 444-3671
Alaska	(907) 465-5152	Nebraska	(402) 471-2451
Arkansas	(501) 661-2534	Nevada	(702) 687-6615
Arizona	(602) 542-7307	New Hampshire	(603) 271-4507
California	(510) 450-2424	New Jersey	(609) 530-8812
Colorado	(303) 692-3012	New Mexico	(505) 841-8024
Connecticut	(203) 566-5808	New York	(518) 473-4602
Washington DC	(202) 727-9850	North Carolina	(919) 715-3293
Delaware	(302) 739-4735	North Dakota	(701) 328-5188
Florida	(904) 488-3385	Ohio	(614) 466-1450
Georgia	(404) 657-6514	Oklahoma	(405) 271-5220
Hawaii	(808) 832-5860	Oregon	(503) 248-5240
Idaho	(208) 332-5544	Pennsylvania	(717) 782-2884
Illinois	(800) 545-2200	Puerto Rico	(809) 766-2823
Indiana	(317) 382-6662	Rhode Island	(401) 277-3424
Iowa	(800) 972-2026	South Carolina	(803) 935-7945
Kansas	(913) 296-0189	South Dakota	(605) 773-3153
Kentucky	(502) 564-2154	Tennessee	(615) 741-5683
Louisiana	(504) 765-0219	Texas	(512) 834-6600
Massachusetts	(800) 532-9571	Utah	(801) 536-4000
Maryland	(410) 631-3859	Vermont	(802) 863-7231
Maine	(207) 287-4311	Virginia	(800) 523-4019
Michigan	(517) 335-8885	Washington	(206) 753-2556
Minnesota	(612) 627-5498	West Virginia	(304) 558-2981
Mississippi	(601) 960-7463	Wisconsin	(608) 266-5885
Missouri	(314) 526-4911	Wyoming	(307) 777-7391

Para Más Información

El Centro Nacional de Información Sobre Plomo

Llame al 1-800-532-3394 para obtener información sobre cómo proteger a los niños del envenenamiento de plomo.

Para obtener información adicional sobre peligros del plomo, llame a la oficina del Centro, al 1-800-424-5323, o TDD 1-800-526-5456 para los que tienen problemas para oir. (FAX: 202-659-1192, Internet: EHC@CAIS.COM).

Teléfono Especial de la EPA para Agua de Beber Segura

Llame al 1-800-426-4761 para obtener información sobre plomo en el agua de beber.

Teléfono Especial de la Comisión de Seguridad de Productos de Consumo

Para pedir información sobre el plomo en productos de consumo, o para reportar que un producto para el consumo es peligroso o una lesión relacionada con un producto, llame al 1-800-638-2772. (Internet: info@cpsc.gov). Las personas que tienen problemas para oir, pueden llamar al 1-800-638-8720.

Fuentes Locales de Información:

Pasos Sencillos Para Proteger a Su Familia de los Peligros del Plomo

Si usted cree que su casa tiene altos niveles de plomo:

- Lleve a sus niños para que les hagan exámenes para plomo, aunque parezcan saludables.

- Lave las manos, botellas y chupetes de los niños frecuentemente.

- Asegúrese que los niños coman alimentos sanos y bajos en grasa.

- Haga que revisen su casa para ver si hay peligros del plomo.

- Limpie los pisos, las molduras de las ventanas y otras superficies frecuentemente.

- Quítele la tierra a los zapatos antes de entrar en la casa.

- Hable con el propietario que le alquila a usted sobre el arreglo de las superficies que tienen pintura que se esté pelando o quebrando.

- Tome precauciones para evitar la exposición al polvo de plomo cuando esté remodelando o renovando (llame al 1-800-424-5323 para obtener orientaciones).

- No use una lijadora de cinta, soplete de propano, raspadora en seco o papel de lija en seco en las superficies que pudieran contener plomo.

- No trate usted mismo(a) de quitar la pintura a base de plomo.

Oficinas Regionales de la EPA

Su contacto Regional de la EPA puede proporcionar más información sobre regulaciones y programas de envenenamiento de plomo que le afecten a usted.

Oficinas Regionales de la EPA

Región 1 (Connecticut, Massachusetts, Maine, New Hampshire, Rhode Island, Vermont)
John F. Kennedy Federal Building
One Congress Street
Boston, MA 02203
(617) 565-3420

Región 2 (New Jersey, New York, Puerto Rico, Virgin Islands)
2890 Woodbridge Avenue
Building 5
Edison, NJ 08837-3679
(908) 321-6671

Región 3 (Delaware, Washington DC, Maryland, Pennsylvania, Virginia, West Virginia)
841 Chestnut Building
Philadelphia, PA 19107
(215) 597-9800

Región 4 (Alabama, Florida, Georgia, Kentucky, Mississippi, North Carolina, South Carolina, Tennessee)
345 Courtland Street, NE
Atlanta, GA 30365
(404) 347-4727

Región 5 (Illinois, Indiana, Michigan, Minnesota, Ohio, Wisconsin)
77 West Jackson Boulevard
Chicago, IL 60604-3590
(312) 886-6003

Región 6 (Arkansas, Louisiana, New Mexico, Oklahoma, Texas)
First Interstate Bank Tower
1445 Ross Avenue, 12th Floor, Suite 1200
Dallas, TX 75202-2733
(214) 665-7244

Región 7 (Iowa, Kansas, Missouri, Nebraska)
726 Minnesota Avenue
Kansas City, KS 66101
(913) 551-7020

Región 8 (Colorado, Montana, North Dakota, South Dakota, Utah, Wyoming)
999 18th Street, Suite 500
Denver, CO 80202-2405
(303) 293-1603

Región 9 (Arizona, California, Hawaii, Nevada)
75 Hawthorne Street
San Francisco, CA 94105
(415) 744-1124

Región 10 (Idaho, Oregon, Washington, Alaska)
1200 Sixth Avenue
Seattle, WA 98101
(206) 553-1200

Oficinas Regionales de CPSC

Centro Regional del Este
6 World Trade Center
Vesey Street, Room 350
New York, NY 10048
(212) 466-1612

Centro Regional Central
230 South Dearborn Street
Room 2944
Chicago, IL 60604-1601
(312) 353-8260

Centro Regional del Oeste
600 Harrison Street, Room 245
San Francisco, CA 94107
(415) 744-2966

Rental Application

SEPARATE APPLICATION REQUIRED FROM EACH APPLICANT AGE 18 OR OLDER.

THIS SECTION TO BE COMPLETED BY LANDLORD

Address of Property to Be Rented: _____

Rental Term: ☐ month-to-month ☐ lease from _____ to _____

Amounts Due Prior to Occupancy

First month's rent .... $ _____

Security deposit .... $ _____

Credit check fee .... $ _____

Other (specify): _____ $ _____

TOTAL .... $ _____

APPLICANT

Full Name—include all names you use(d):_____

Home Phone: (_____)_____ Work Phone: (_____)_____

Social Security Number:_____ Driver's License Number/State:_____

Other Identifying Information:_____

Vehicle Make:_____ Model:_____ Color:_____ Year:_____

License Plate Number/State:_____

ADDITIONAL OCCUPANTS

List everyone, including children, who will live with you:

Full Name	Relationship to Applicant

RENTAL HISTORY

Current Address:_____

Dates Lived at Address:_____ Reason for Leaving: _____

Landlord/Manager:_____ Landlord/Manager's Phone: (_____)_____

Previous Address:_____

Dates Lived at Address: _____ Reason for Leaving: _____

Landlord/Manager: _____ Landlord/Manager's Phone: (_____)_____

Previous Address:_____

Dates Lived at Address: _____ Reason for Leaving: _____

EMPLOYMENT HISTORY

Name and Address of Current Employer:_____

_____ Phone:(_____)_____

Name of Supervisor:_____ Supervisor's Phone:(_____)_____

Dates Employed at This Job:_____ Position or Title:_____

Name and Address of Previous Employer:_____

_____ Phone:(_____)_____

Name of Supervisor:_____ Supervisor's Phone:(_____)_____

Dates Employed at This Job:_____ Position or Title:_____

INCOME

1. Your gross monthly employment income (before deductions): $ _____

2. Average monthly amounts of other income (specify sources): $ _____

_____

_____

TOTAL: $ _____

CREDIT AND FINANCIAL INFORMATION

Bank/Financial Accounts	Account Number	Bank/Institution	Branch
Savings Account:			
Checking Account:			
Money Market or Similar Account:			

Credit Accounts & Loans	Type of Account (Auto loan, Visa, etc.)	Account Number	Name of Creditor	Amount Owed	Monthly Payment
Major Credit Card:					
Major Credit Card:					
Loan (mortgage, car, student loan, etc.):					
Other Major Obligations:					

MISCELLANEOUS

Describe the number and type of pets you want to have in the rental property:

Describe water-filled furniture you want to have in the rental property:

Do you smoke? ☐ yes ☐ no

Have you ever: Filed for bankruptcy? ☐ yes ☐ no   Been sued? ☐ yes ☐ no

   Been evicted? ☐ yes ☐ no   Been convicted of a crime? ☐ yes ☐ no

Explain any "yes" listed above:

REFERENCES AND EMERGENCY CONTACT

Personal Reference:_____ Relationship:_____

Address:_____

_____ Phone: (_____)_____

Personal Reference:_____ Relationship:_____

Address:_____

_____ Phone: (_____)_____

Contact in Emergency:_____ Relationship:_____

Address:_____

_____ Phone: (_____)_____

I certify that all the information given above is true and correct and understand that my lease or rental agreement may be terminated if I have made any material false or incomplete statements in this application. I authorize verification of the information provided in this application from my credit sources, credit bureaus, current and previous landlords and employers, and personal references.

_____   _____

Date   Applicant

Notes (Landlord/Manager):_____

_____

_____

_____

_____

_____

_____

_____

_____

_____

Consent to Background and Reference Check

I authorize _____ to obtain information about me

from my credit sources, credit bureaus, current and previous landlords and employers and personal

references. I authorize my credit sources, credit bureaus, current and previous landlords and employers

and personal references to disclose to _____

_____ such information about me that is relevant to

_____'s evaluation of me as a prospective tenant.

_____

Name

_____

Address

_____

Phone Number

_____

Date   Applicant

Tenant References

Name of Applicant: _____

Address of Rental Unit: _____

PREVIOUS LANDLORD OR MANAGER

Contact (name, property owner or manager, address of rental unit): _____

_____

Date: _____

QUESTIONS

When did tenant rent from you (move-in and move-out dates)? _____

What was the monthly rent? _____ Did tenant pay rent on time? _____

Was tenant considerate of neighbors—that is, no loud parties and fair, careful use of common areas?

_____

Did tenant have any pets? If so, were there any problems? _____

_____

Did tenant make any unreasonable demands or complaints? _____

_____

Why did tenant leave? _____

_____

Did tenant give the proper amount of notice before leaving?_____

Did tenant leave the place in good condition? Did you need to use the security deposit to cover damage?

_____

Any particular problems you'd like to mention?_____

_____

_____

Would you rent to this person again? _____

_____

Other Comments: _____

_____

_____

_____

_____

_____

_____

EMPLOYMENT VERIFICATION

Contact (name, company, position):_____

Date:_____ Salary:_____ Dates of Employment:_____

Comments:_____

_____

_____

_____

_____

_____

_____

PERSONAL REFERENCE

Contact (name and relationship to applicant):_____

Date:_____ How long have you known the applicant?_____

Would you recommend this person as a prospective tenant?_____

Comments:_____

_____

_____

_____

_____

_____

CREDIT AND FINANCIAL INFORMATION

_____

_____

_____

_____

NOTES (INCLUDING REASONS FOR REJECTING APPLICANT)

_____

_____

_____

_____

_____

_____

_____

_____

Notice of Denial Based on Credit Report Information

To: _____
    Applicant

_____
    Street Address

_____
    City, State and Zip Code

THIS NOTICE is to inform you that your application to rent the property at _____

_____

[*rental property address*] has been denied because of [*check all that apply*]:

☐ Insufficient information in the credit report provided by _____

_____

[*name, address and telephone number of consumer credit reporting agency providing credit report; including toll-free telephone number if this is a national credit reporting agency*]

☐ Negative information in the credit report provided by _____

_____

[*name, address and telephone number of consumer credit reporting agency providing credit report; including toll-free telephone number if this is a national credit reporting agency*]

The consumer credit reporting agency noted above did not make the decision not to rent to you and cannot explain why your application was rejected. It only provided information about your credit history.

Providing this notice meets the requirements of the federal Fair Credit Reporting Act (15 U.S.C. §§ 1681 and following). You have the right under this Act to obtain a free copy of your credit report from the consumer credit reporting agency named above, if your request is made within 60 days of this notice (15 U.S.C. § 1681j). You also have the right to dispute the accuracy or completeness of your credit report and add your own "consumer statement" (up to 100 words) to the report (15 U.S.C. § 1681i). For more information, contact the above-named consumer credit reporting agency.

_____   _____

Date   Owner/Manager

Landlord/Tenant Checklist

GENERAL CONDITION OF ROOMS

Street Address _____ Unit Number ____ City _____

	Condition on Arrival	Condition on Departure	Estimated Cost of Repair/Replacement
LIVING ROOM			
Floors & Floor Coverings			
Drapes & Window Coverings			
Walls & Ceilings			
Light Fixtures			
Windows, Screens & Doors			
Front Door & Locks			
Fireplace			
Other			
Other			
KITCHEN			
Floors & Floor Coverings			
Walls & Ceilings			
Light Fixtures			
Cabinets			
Counters			
Stove/Oven			
Refrigerator			
Dishwasher			
Garbage Disposal			
Sink & Plumbing			
Windows, Screens & Doors			
Other			
Other			
DINING ROOM			
Floors & Floor Covering			
Walls & Ceiling			
Light Fixtures			
Windows, Screens & Doors			

	Condition on Arrival		Condition on Departure		Estimated Cost of Repair/Replacement
Other					
Other					
BATHROOM(S)	Bath 1	Bath 2	Bath 1	Bath 2	
Floors & Floor Coverings					
Walls & Ceilings					
Windows, Screens & Doors					
Light Fixtures					
Bathtub/Shower					
Sink & Counters					
Toilet					
Other					
Other					
BEDROOM(S)	Bdrm 1	Bdrm 2	Bdrm 3	Bdrm 1	Bdrm 2 Bdrm 3
Floors & Floor Coverings					
Windows, Screens & Doors					
Walls & Ceilings					
Light Fixtures					
Other					
Other					
OTHER AREAS					
Heating System					
Air Conditioning					
Lawn/Garden					
Stairs & Hallway					
Patio, Terrace, Deck, etc.					
Basement					
Parking Area					
Other					
Other					

☐ Tenants acknowledge that all smoke detectors and fire extinguishers were tested in their presence and found to be in working order, and that the testing procedure was explained to them. Tenants agree to test all detectors at least once a month and to report any problems to Landlord/Manager in writing. Tenants agree to replace all smoke detector batteries as necessary.

FURNISHED PROPERTY

	Condition on Arrival	Condition on Departure	Estimated Cost of Repair/Replacement
LIVING ROOM			
Coffee Table			
End Tables			
Lamps			
Chairs			
Sofa			
Other			
Other			
KITCHEN			
Broiler Pan			
Ice Trays			
Other			
Other			
DINING AREA			
Chairs			
Stools			
Table			
Other			
Other			
BATHROOM(S)	Bath 1 Bath 2	Bath 1 Bath 2	
Mirrors			
Shower Curtain			
Hamper			
Other			
Other			
BEDROOM(S)	Bdrm 1 Bdrm 2 Bdrm 3	Bdrm 1 Bdrm 2 Bdrm 3	
Beds (single)			
Beds (double)			
Chairs			
Chests			
Dressing Tables			
Lamps			
Mirrors			
Night Tables			
Other			
Other			

	Condition on Arrival	Condition on Departure	Estimated Cost of Repair/Replacement
Other			
OTHER AREAS			
Bookcases			
Desks			
Pictures			
Other			
Other			

Use this space to provide any additional explanation:

_____

_____

_____

_____

_____

_____

_____

_____

_____

_____

_____

_____

Landlord/Tenant Checklist completed on moving in on _____, 200____ and approved by:

_____ and _____
Landlord/Manager   Tenant

_____
Tenant

_____
Tenant

Landlord/Tenant Checklist completed on moving out on _____, 200____ and approved by:

_____ and _____
Landlord/Manager   Tenant

_____
Tenant

_____
Tenant

Move-In Letter

_____ (date)

_____ (tenant)

_____ (street address)

_____ (city and state)

Dear _____ , (tenant)

Welcome to _____

_____ (address of rental unit). We hope you will enjoy living here. This letter is to

explain what you can expect from the management and what we'll be looking for from you:

1. **Rent:** _____

_____ .

2. **New Roommates:** _____

_____

_____

_____ .

3. **Notice to End Tenancy:** _____

_____

_____ .

4. **Deposits:**

_____

_____

_____ .

5. **Manager:** _____

_____

_____ .

6. **Landlord-Tenant Checklist:** _____

_____

_____

_____

_____

7. **Maintenance/Repair Problems:** _____
_____
_____
_____
_____
_____

8. **Semi-Annual Safety and Maintenance Update** _____
_____
_____

9. **Annual Safety Inspection:** _____
_____
_____

10. **Insurance:** _____
_____
_____
_____
_____

11. **Moving Out:** _____
_____
_____
_____
_____

12. **Telephone Number Changes:** _____
_____

Please let us know if you have any questions.

Sincerely,

_____   _____
Date   Owner

I have read and received a copy of this statement.

_____   _____
Date   Tenant

Tenant's Notice of Intent to Move Out

_____ (date)

_____ (landlord/manager)

_____ (street address)

_____ (city and state)

Dear _____ , (landlord/manager)

This is to notify you that the undersigned tenant(s) _____

_____

_____ will be moving from

_____ ,

on _____ , or

_____ from today. This provides at

least _____ written notice as required in our rental agreement.

Sincerely,

_____

Tenant

_____

Tenant

_____

Tenant

Move-Out Letter

_____ (date)

_____ (tenant)

_____ (street address)

_____ (city and state)

Dear _____ , (tenant)

We hope you have enjoyed living here. In order that we may mutually end our relationship on a positive note, this move-out letter describes how we expect your unit to be left and what our procedures are for returning your security deposit.

Basically, we expect you to leave your rental unit in the same condition it was when you moved in, except for normal wear and tear. To refresh your memory on the condition of the unit when you moved in, I've attached a copy of the Landlord/Tenant Checklist you signed at the beginning of your tenancy. I'll be using this same form to inspect your unit when you leave.

Specifically, here's a list of items you should thoroughly clean before vacating:

☐ Floors

    ☐ sweep wood floors

    ☐ vacuum carpets and rugs (shampoo if necessary)

    ☐ mop kitchen and bathroom floors

☐ Walls, baseboards, ceilings and built-in shelves

☐ Kitchen cabinets, countertops and sink, stove and oven—inside and out

☐ Refrigerator—clean inside and out, empty it of food and turn it off

☐ Bathtubs, showers, toilets and plumbing fixtures

☐ Doors, windows and window coverings

☐ Other _____

_____

_____

_____

_____

_____

_____

_____

_____

_____

_____

If you have any questions as to the type of cleaning we expect, please let me know.

Please don't leave *anything* behind—that includes bags of garbage, clothes, food, newspapers, furniture, appliances, dishes, plants, cleaning supplies or other items belonging to you.

Please be sure you have disconnected phone and utility services, canceled all newspaper subscriptions and sent the post office a change-of-address form.

Once you have cleaned your unit and removed *all* your belongings, please call me at

_____ to arrange for a walk-through inspection and to return all keys. Please be prepared to give me your forwarding address where we may mail your security deposit.

It's our policy to return all deposits either in person or at an address you provide within _____ after you move out. If any deductions are made—for past due rent or because the unit is damaged or not sufficiently clean—they will be explained in writing.

If you have any questions, please contact me at _____.

Sincerely,

_____

Landlord/Manager

Index

CATALOG

...more from Nolo

	PRICE	CODE

BUSINESS

	PRICE	CODE
The CA Nonprofit Corporation Kit (Binder w/CD-ROM)	$59.95	CNP
Consultant & Independent Contractor Agreements (Book w/CD-ROM)	$29.95	CICA
The Corporate Minutes Book (Book w/CD-ROM)	$69.99	CORMI
The Employer's Legal Handbook	$39.99	EMPL
Everyday Employment Law	$29.99	ELBA
Drive a Modest Car & 16 Other Keys to Small Business Sucess	$24.99	DRIV
Form Your Own Limited Liability Company (Book w/CD-ROM)	$44.99	LIAB
Hiring Independent Contractors: The Employer's Legal Guide (Book w/CD-ROM)	$34.99	HICI
How to Create a Buy-Sell Agreement & Control the Destiny of your Small Business (Book w/Disk-PC)	$49.95	BSAG
How to Create a Noncompete Agreement	$44.95	NOCMP
How to Form a California Professional Corporation (Book w/CD-ROM)	$59.95	PROF
How to Form a Nonprofit Corporation (Book w/CD-ROM)—National Edition	$44.99	NNP
How to Form a Nonprofit Corporation in California (Book w/CD-ROM)	$44.99	NON
How to Form Your Own California Corporation (Binder w/CD-ROM)	$59.99	CACI
How to Form Your Own California Corporation (Book w/CD-ROM)	$34.99	CCOR
How to Get Your Business on the Web	$29.99	WEBS
How to Write a Business Plan	$34.99	SBS
The Independent Paralegal's Handbook	$29.95	PARA
Leasing Space for Your Small Business	$34.95	LESP
Legal Guide for Starting & Running a Small Business	$34.99	RUNS
Legal Forms for Starting & Running a Small Business (Book w/CD-ROM)	$29.95	RUNS2
Marketing Without Advertising	$24.00	MWAD
Music Law (Book w/CD-ROM)	$34.99	ML
Nolo's Guide to Social Security Disability	$29.99	QSS
Nolo's Quick LLC	$24.99	LLCQ
Nondisclosure Agreements	$39.95	NAG
The Small Business Start-up Kit (Book w/CD-ROM)	$29.99	SMBU
The Small Business Start-up Kit for California (Book w/CD-ROM)	$34.99	OPEN
The Partnership Book: How to Write a Partnership Agreement (Book w/CD-ROM)	$39.99	PART
Sexual Harassment on the Job	$24.95	HARS
Starting & Running a Successful Newsletter or Magazine	$29.99	MAG

Prices subject to change.

	PRICE	CODE
Tax Savvy for Small Business	$34.99	SAVVY
Working for Yourself: Law & Taxes for the Self-Employed	$39.99	WAGE
Your Crafts Business: A Legal Guide	$26.99	VART
Your Limited Liability Company: An Operating Manual (Book w/CD-ROM)	$49.99	LOP
Your Rights in the Workplace	$29.99	YRW

CONSUMER

	PRICE	CODE
How to Win Your Personal Injury Claim	$29.99	PICL
Nolo's Encyclopedia of Everyday Law	$29.99	EVL
Nolo's Guide to California Law	$24.95	CLAW
Trouble-Free Travel...And What to Do When Things Go Wrong	$14.95	TRAV

ESTATE PLANNING & PROBATE

	PRICE	CODE
8 Ways to Avoid Probate	$19.95	PRO8
9 Ways to Avoid Estate Taxes	$29.95	ESTX
Estate Planning Basics	$21.99	ESPN
How to Probate an Estate in California	$49.99	PAE
Make Your Own Living Trust (Book w/CD-ROM)	$39.99	LITR
Nolo's Law Form Kit: Wills	$24.95	KWL
Nolo's Simple Will Book (Book w/CD-ROM)	$34.99	SWIL
Plan Your Estate	$44.99	NEST
Quick & Legal Will Book	$15.99	QUIC

FAMILY MATTERS

	PRICE	CODE
Child Custody: Building Parenting Agreements That Work	$29.95	CUST
The Complete IEP Guide	$24.99	IEP
Divorce & Money: How to Make the Best Financial Decisions During Divorce	$34.99	DIMO
Get a Life: You Don't Need a Million to Retire Well	$24.99	LIFE
The Guardianship Book for California	$39.99	GB
How to Adopt Your Stepchild in California (Book w/CD-ROM)	$34.95	ADOP
A Legal Guide for Lesbian and Gay Couples	$29.99	LG
Living Together: A Legal Guide (Book w/CD-ROM)	$34.99	LTK
Using Divorce Mediation: Save Your Money & Your Sanity	$29.95	UDMD

GOING TO COURT

	PRICE	CODE
Beat Your Ticket: Go To Court and Win! (National Edition)	$19.99	BEYT
The Criminal Law Handbook: Know Your Rights, Survive the System	$34.99	KYR
Everybody's Guide to Small Claims Court (National Edition)	$26.99	NSCC
Everybody's Guide to Small Claims Court in California	$26.99	CSCC

	PRICE	CODE

MONEY MATTERS

	PRICE	CODE
101 Law Forms for Personal Use (Book w/CD-ROM)	$29.99	SPOT
Bankruptcy: Is It the Right Solution to Your Debt Problems?	$19.99	BRS
Chapter 13 Bankruptcy: Repay Your Debts	$34.99	CH13
Creating Your Own Retirement Plan	$29.99	YROP
Credit Repair (Quick & Legal Series, Book w/CD-ROM)	$24.99	CREP
How to File for Chapter 7 Bankruptcy	$34.99	HFB
IRAs, 401(k)s & Other Retirement Plans: Taking Your Money Out	$34.99	RET
Money Troubles: Legal Strategies to Cope With Your Debts	$29.99	MT
Nolo's Law Form Kit: Personal Bankruptcy	$24.99	KBNK
Stand Up to the IRS	$24.99	SIRS
Surviving an IRS Tax Audit	$24.95	SAUD
Take Control of Your Student Loan Debt	$26.95	SLOAN

PATENTS AND COPYRIGHTS

	PRICE	CODE
The Copyright Handbook: How to Protect and Use Written Works (Book w/CD-ROM)	$39.99	COHA
Copyright Your Software	$34.95	CYS
Domain Names	$26.95	DOM
Getting Permission: How to License and Clear Copyrighted Materials Online and Off (Book w/CD-ROM)	$34.99	RIPER
How to Make Patent Drawings Yourself	$29.99	DRAW
The Inventor's Notebook	$24.99	INOT
Nolo's Patents for Beginners	$29.99	QPAT
License Your Invention (Book w/CD-ROM)	$39.99	LICE
Patent, Copyright & Trademark	$39.99	PCTM
Patent It Yourself	$49.99	PAT
Patent Searching Made Easy	$29.95	PATSE
The Public Domain	$34.95	PUBL
Web and Software Development: A Legal Guide (Book w/ CD-ROM)	$44.95	SFT
Trademark: Legal Care for Your Business and Product Name	$39.95	TRD

RESEARCH & REFERENCE

	PRICE	CODE
Legal Research: How to Find & Understand the Law	$34.99	LRES

SENIORS

	PRICE	CODE
Choose the Right Long-Term Care: Home Care, Assisted Living & Nursing Homes	$21.99	ELD
The Conservatorship Book for California	$44.99	CNSV
Social Security, Medicare & Goverment Pensions	$29.99	SOA

SOFTWARE

**Call or check our website at www.nolo.com
for special discounts on Software!**

LeaseWriter CD—Windows $129.95   LWD1

LLC Maker—Windows $89.95   LLP1

PatentPro Plus—Windows .... $399.99   PAPL

Personal RecordKeeper 5.0 CD—Windows $59.95   RKD5

Quicken Lawyer 2003 Business Deluxe—Windows $79.95   SBQB3

Quicken Lawyer 2003 Personal—Windows $79.95   WQP3

Special
Upgrade Offer

Save 35% on the latest edition of your Nolo book

Because laws and legal procedures change often, we update our books regularly. To help keep you up-to-date, we are extending this special upgrade offer. Cut out and mail the title portion of the cover of your old Nolo book and we'll give you **35% off** the retail price of the NEW EDITION of that book when you purchase directly from Nolo. This offer is to individuals only.

Call us today at 1-800-728-3555

Prices and offer subject to change without notice.

Order Form

Name

Address

City

State, Zip

Daytime Phone

E-mail

Our "No-Hassle" Guarantee

Return anything you buy directly from Nolo for any reason and we'll cheerfully refund your purchase price. No ifs, ands or buts.

☐ Check here if you do not wish to receive mailings from other companies

Item Code	Quantity	Item	Unit Price	Total Price

Method of payment

☐ Check ☐ VISA ☐ MasterCard
☐ Discover Card ☐ American Express

Subtotal	
Add your local sales tax (California only)	
Shipping: RUSH $9, Basic $5 (See below)	
"I bought 3, ship it to me FREE!"(Ground shipping only)	
TOTAL	

Account Number

Expiration Date

Signature

Shipping and Handling

Rush Delivery—Only $9

We'll ship any order to any street address in the U.S. by UPS 2nd Day Air* for only $9!

* Order by noon Pacific Time and get your order in 2 business days. Orders placed after noon Pacific Time will arrive in 3 business days. P.O. boxes and S.F. Bay Area use basic shipping. Alaska and Hawaii use 2nd Day Air or Priority Mail.

Basic Shipping—$5

Use for P.O. Boxes, Northern California and Ground Service.

Allow 1-2 weeks for delivery. U.S. addresses only.

For faster service, use your credit card and our toll-free numbers

**Call our customer service group
Monday thru Friday 7am to 7pm PST**

Phone	1-800-728-3555
Fax	1-800-645-0895
Mail	Nolo
950 Parker St.
Berkeley, CA 94710

**Order 24 hours a day @
www.nolo.com**

Remember:

Little publishers have big ears.
We really listen to you.

Take 2 Minutes & Give Us Your 2 cents

Your comments make a big difference in the development and revision of Nolo books and software. Please take a few minutes and register your Nolo product—and your comments—with us. Not only will your input make a difference, you'll receive special offers available only to registered owners of Nolo products on our newest books and software. Register now by:

PHONE
1-800-728-3555

FAX
1-800-645-0895

EMAIL
cs@nolo.com

or **MAIL** us
this registration card

fold here

Registration Card

NAME _____ DATE _____

ADDRESS _____

_____

CITY _____ STATE _____ ZIP _____

PHONE _____ E-MAIL _____

WHERE DID YOU HEAR ABOUT THIS PRODUCT? _____

WHERE DID YOU PURCHASE THIS PRODUCT? _____

DID YOU CONSULT A LAWYER? (PLEASE CIRCLE ONE)   YES   NO   NOT APPLICABLE

DID YOU FIND THIS BOOK HELPFUL?   (VERY)   5   4   3   2   1   (NOT AT ALL)

COMMENTS _____

_____

_____

WAS IT EASY TO USE?   (VERY EASY)   5   4   3   2   1   (VERY DIFFICULT)

We occasionally make our mailing list available to carefully selected companies whose products may be of interest to you.

❏   If you do not wish to receive mailings from these companies, please check this box.

❏   You can quote me in future Nolo promotional materials.
Daytime phone number _____.

LEAR 4.0

"Nolo helps lay people perform legal tasks without the aid—or fees—of lawyers."

—USA TODAY

Nolo books are ...*"written in plain language, free of legal mumbo jumbo, and spiced with witty personal observations."*

—ASSOCIATED PRESS

"...Nolo publications...guide people simply through the how, when, where and why of law."

—WASHINGTON POST

"Increasingly, people who are not lawyers are performing tasks usually regarded as legal work... And consumers, using books like Nolo's, do routine legal work themselves."

—NEW YORK TIMES

"...All of [Nolo's] books are easy-to-understand, are updated regularly, provide pull-out forms...and are often quite moving in their sense of compassion for the struggles of the lay reader."

—SAN FRANCISCO CHRONICLE

- - - - - - - - - - - - - - - - - - fold here -

> **Place
> stamp here**

 **Nolo**
950 Parker Street
Berkeley, CA 94710-9867

Attn: | **LEAR 4.0** |